CHRIST
Our Passover

CHRIST
Our Passover

The Indispensable
Role of Resurrection
in Our Salvation

FRANCIS XAVIER DURRWELL, C.SS.R.
TRANSLATED BY JOHN F. CRAGHAN

Liguori

LIGUORI, MISSOURI

Imprimi Potest:
Richard Thibodeau, C.Ss.R.
Provincial, Denver Province
The Redemptorists

Imprimatur:
October 18, 2000, Feast of Saint Luke the Evangelist
A. Kiefer, Archbishop of Strasbourg

Translation copyright © 2004 by John F. Craghan
Library of Congress Control Number: 2003114057

Previously published as *Christ Notre Pâque* by Nouvelle Cité in Montrouge, France, 2001.

Except where noted, Scripture citations are taken from the *New Revised Standard Version of the Bible,* copyright 1989 by the Division of Christian Education of the National Council of the Churches of Christ in the USA. All rights reserved. Used with permission. Noted Scripture citations [NAB] are taken from the *New American Bible,* copyright 1970, 1986, and 1991 by the Confraternity of Christian Doctrine, Washington, D.C., and are used with permission. All rights reserved.

Printed in the United States of America
08 07 06 05 04   5 4 3 2 1
Translation edition 2004

*E*very sin that a person commits contradicts the resurrection of Jesus. All the errors or deficiencies that one can deplore in theology are due, in part at least, to the lack of or to the little attention paid to the resurrection of Jesus. In Christian thought, as in life, the link to the resurrection is the determining factor.

Easter, 2000

CONTENTS

Contents

PREFACE

I was born in an area where, as opposed to the rest of France, Good Friday is a holiday. In the morning the bells of the Protestant churches began to ring, the Last Supper was celebrated, "you proclaim the Lord's death" (1 Cor 11:26), and the remission of sins was announced. The bells of the Catholic churches, however, waited in silence until the joy of "*Gloria in excelsis Deo*" burst forth during the Easter Vigil.[1] Two distinct theologies were articulated over the roofs of that city: (1) salvation acquired at the price of Christ's death and (2) salvation realized in Christ through his death *and* his resurrection.

I took theology courses in the seminary and from Catholic university faculties until 1940. No one taught me the theology that is signified by the Easter Vigil liturgy. I never heard the phrase "paschal mystery" uttered. The teaching in those places was hardly different from the churches of the Reformation.

Only later did I realize how this teaching was split up. There was no link that bound the great disciplines together: dogmatic theology, moral theology, spirituality, or church law. In studying dogmatic theology a great autonomy prevailed among the tracts. One began with "*de Deo uno*" followed by "*de Deo trino*." The unity of God rested on the mystery of the Trinity. In Christology, the second part "*de Christo redemptore*" was connected to the first part "*de Verbo Incarnato*," because it was held that to pay the infinite price of redemption, Jesus needed to be both human and divine.

The fact that he was both human and the Son of God was of no further consequence. In sacramental theology, for example, it was hard to perceive the unity of the Eucharist: sacrament of presence and sacrament of sacrifice.

Such was the case in almost everything. We had thus removed the keystone from the wonderful cathedral of revealed mystery where every piece comprises the whole and each element has meaning by being integrated into that whole. What remains of a building whose keystone has been removed? The scattered stones retain their singular beauty, but it is only in the whole reality that each one plays its role.

The keystone that is also the foundation stone is Christ raised from the dead. In that period of history we placed all the weight of redemption on Jesus' death alone. We emphasized the resurrection only in apologetics. It was seen as the proof of faith by which humanity is justified. One underlined the resurrection's exemplary value, too: raised from the dead, Jesus is the image of the justified person because of the blood of the cross. It is in these two senses that we interpreted the phrase, "who was raised for our justification" (Rom 4:25). We did not take into account the text, "And if Christ has not been raised, then our proclamation is in vain and your faith has been in vain...and if Christ has not been raised, your faith is futile and you are still in your sins" (1 Cor 15:14, 17). In 1948, a specialist recognized in the theology of redemption wrote, "Everything one can say about the resurrection, ascension, and sacraments is only accessory to the real subject."[2]

Toward the end of my seminary training (1937), I became certain that Christ's Resurrection, together with his death, forms part of the mystery of redemption. One morning in February

1940, I finally understood what I had been sure was true. Reading Galatians 4:1–6, I became aware of the reality beneath that text, of what is written between the lines, and of what this book will attempt to show once again, that redemption is the personal mystery of Jesus, his drama as Man/Son of God who, born in solidarity with sinful humanity, entered into his filial fullness with the Father through his death. Jesus not only merited the salvation of humanity at the cost of his sufferings—in his death and his resurrection he became the salvation of the world that humans are called to enter. "By him [God] you were called into the fellowship of (*sic.* communion with) his Son" (1 Cor 1:9).

Quickly and by itself the cathedral was rebuilt before my very eyes in its harmonious beauty. If the salvation of the world is realized in Christ's death *and* resurrection, then Jesus is *in person* the eschatological mystery, the kingdom of God that was announced. In order to be saved, humans enter through faith into communion with him, forming with him one single body that is the Church. They share in his death and resurrection for their salvation and for the salvation of the world. The Christian life is a celebration of communion with Christ in his Passover. The sacraments nourish this life of paschal communion. The entire cathedral is illuminated by the Trinitarian mystery revealed in Jesus whom the Father begets to his filial fullness by raising him in the power of the Holy Spirit.

After the grief of World War II and the difficult postwar years, I was finally able to publish *The Resurrection of Jesus, Mystery of Salvation* (1950). Other works followed, all of which treated the same subject. In this present book the desire was awakened to bring together the elements scattered in those works, to bundle the sheaves, and make of them "the evening offering." This desire is accompanied with the fear, greater than in the past, of not being up to the task. Is one ever up to any task before the mystery realized and revealed in Jesus Christ? One can only look at the sun through dark glasses. God willing, mine are not warped.

I wish to express my heartfelt thanks to Sonia and Brother Patrick who have reworked my notes. Without their devotion this work could never have seen the light of day.[3]

Chapter One

THE END WHERE EVERYTHING BEGINS

The Resurrection is the final stage. It was for Jesus, and it will be for the Church. The history of Jesus and the Church was accomplished in the Resurrection. However, everything begins there for both Jesus and the Church, as well. Christianity derives its source precisely where it finds its ultimate achievement.

For the Church, the paradox of an end where everything begins is not surprising. Jesus called himself "the resurrection" (Jn 11:25), projecting that event to the last day (cf. Jn 5:25). According to Saint Paul the Resurrection of Jesus was the "resurrection of the dead" (Rom 1:4) [NAB].[4] The history of the Church will be accomplished by its shared encounter with Christ in his Resurrection. It was also in that encounter that the Church was born. Rising, Jesus lives again and becomes a great crowd—he became a Church—like a grain of wheat that produces much fruit (cf. Jn 12:24). He rose as spouse of a Church that did not exist before his wedding (cf. Eph 5:25–27). The Church is married to him by sharing the resurrection with him in death.

God begot his son in glory—"by raising Jesus; as also it is written in the second psalm, 'You are my Son; today I have begotten you'" (Acts 13:33). At the same time he begot "the Church, which is his body" (Eph 1:19–23). The Church was "made...alive together with Christ" (Eph 2:5)[5] who is the resurrection of the dead, the Lord of the last day. Thus the Church finds its origin in the future to which it is called, "You were called into the fellowship of [communion with] his Son" in his day (1 Cor 1:9). The risen Jesus is the Omega—and the Alpha. By "the power of his resurrection" (Phil 3:10) the Church was called to that resurrection and so lives (cf. 1 Cor 1:9).

Everything began when Jesus rose. "He is risen!" was the cry of the Church at its birth. Faith was stirred up on the day of Easter in the encounter with the Risen One. In our own days it is still set on fire through that encounter. Simon Peter had begun to believe in the messiahship of Jesus, "You are the Messiah" (Mk 8:29). But he refused to accept the death of Jesus (cf. Mk 8:32–33). Peter's faith was not truly Christian. After Jesus' death, faith in him was broken, "We were hoping" is what the disciples on the road to Emmaus reported. "For as yet they did not understand...that he must rise from the dead" (Jn 20:9). But after the Resurrection Peter proclaimed the messiahship of Jesus in all its truth, "God has made him both Lord and Messiah, this Jesus whom you crucified" (Acts 2:36). From then on, having encountered the risen Jesus, he could include Christ's death as part of his faith in the Messiah—Peter was becoming a Christian.

The first communities coined brief statements that sum up their faith. We know several of these formulations of the faith.[6] They are older than the writings of the New Testament that incorporated them into their text. In the year 51 Saint Paul wrote, "For since we believe [he thus proclaimed the formula of faith] that Jesus died and rose again" (1 Thess 4:14).[7] In another pre-Pauline text,[8] the apostle sums up the content of the faith this way, "the gospel about his Son, descended from David according to the flesh, but established as Son of God in power according to the spirit of holiness through resurrection of the dead" (Rom 1:3–4) [NAB]. Here, as in Acts 13:32–33, the gospel is that of the risen Christ. His death is not even mentioned. Notification of his death is contained within the announcement of the risen Christ, who sums up the entire mystery of salvation.

The testimony "Jesus Christ is Lord" (Phil 2:11) also belongs to these hallowed formulas. Jesus became Lord and was recognized as such following his resurrection, "If you confess with your lips that Jesus is Lord and believe in your heart that God raised him from the dead, you will be saved" (Rom 10:9). It was through the power of the Spirit that Jesus was raised (cf. Rom 8:11). It is through the power of that same Spirit that the Christian proclaims his or her faith, "And no one can say, 'Jesus is Lord,' except by the Holy Spirit" (1 Cor 12:3). The faithful believe in the Risen One by the power of the Resurrection.

The apostles were sent by the Risen One and preached by the power which also raised Jesus. "All authority…has been given to me. Go therefore…" (Mt 28:18–19). The power that commissioned the apostles stirred up in them a faith that bore witness, "I believed, and so I spoke" (2 Cor 4:13). But what were they speaking about? Paul has preserved a record of their preaching from what he received at the beginning of his Christian life, "For I handed on to you as of first importance what I in turn had received: that Christ died for our sins in accordance with the scriptures, and that he was buried, and that he was raised on the third day in accordance with the scriptures, and that he appeared to Cephas, then to the twelve" (1 Cor 15:3–5).

Jesus "was handed over to death for our trespasses" (Rom 4:25)[9]—Christ's redemptive death formed part of the early preaching. Its role was important but isolated, for without a connection to the Resurrection, it would be, in the words of Paul, devoid of salvific meaning, "if Christ has not been raised, your faith is futile and you are still in your sins" (1 Cor 15:17).

It would be just what the high priests wanted—his rejection from the nation and from history. Thus no one would speak any more of him.

Yet the resurrection can be proclaimed all by itself.[10] "You will be my witnesses" (Acts 1:8); and witnesses "with us of his resurrection" (Acts 1:22). The resurrection presumes death, sanctions its redemptive meaning, and reveals it. If Paul protests that he wishes to know "only Jesus Christ, and him crucified" (1 Cor 2:2), and if he "proclaim(s) Christ crucified" (1 Cor 1:23), then this Christ is according to him "the Lord of glory" (1 Cor 2:8). But Christ was forever captured by the cross whose power seems to be weakness and whose wisdom is folly in the eyes of humans (cf. 1 Cor 1:17–25).[11] The crucified Christ preached by Paul is the Christ of glory which he became through his death.

The Johannine symbolism synthesizes Christ's death and Resurrection. Being lifted up on a cross symbolizes being lifted above earth into the bosom of God. Raised by the cross into glory, Jesus can draw all people to himself and give them life (cf. Jn 12:32–33). In one movement, it is the end that provides meaning. In some way, the end is first.

The first theme in the disciples' preaching was that the source of faith, the risen Jesus, is the permanent foundation of Christian existence, "your life in Christ Jesus" (1 Cor 1:30). The Pauline formula "in Christ" always designates the Christ of glory. If the believer also shares in Christ's death, it is because such a person is "baptized into Christ" (Rom 6:3), the Christ who is today raised in death. To die with Christ is a grace received by sharing in his resurrection. Similarly, the remission of sins is provided through union with Christ who was "raised for our justification" (Rom 4:25).

The Church was born in the Resurrection of Jesus because Christ, from whom it lives, was himself born in his Passover. The paradox of an end where everything begins, first of all, concerns

4

Jesus himself. It is written in Acts 13:32–33, "We bring you the good news that what God promised to our ancestors he has fulfilled for us, their children, by raising Jesus; as also it is written in the second psalm, 'You are my Son; today I have begotten you.'" A person derives his or her origin from parents who beget him or her. Jesus was begotten by God who raised him from death. In that instant he was born to an eternal today. God raised him in the Holy Spirit and begot him in power (cf. Rom 8:11), and he was "established as Son of God in power according to the spirit of holiness through resurrection of the dead" (Rom 1:4) [NAB]. In his death Jesus rose and was born Son of God in the Holy Spirit.

His earthly birth preceded his birth into the fullness of the Spirit. From his conception, Jesus was the Son in the Holy Spirit: "The Holy Spirit will come upon you [Mary], and the power of the Most High will overshadow you; therefore the child to be born will be called holy; he will be called Son of God" (Lk 1:35). However, the infancy gospels were not written only in the light of Easter—the reports of his birth actually form part of the Passover mystery of Jesus. His birth at Bethlehem anticipated his birth in fullness through the Holy Spirit. In his earthly coming, the mystery that was going to appear was being prepared, similar to the dawn whose light comes from the still hidden sun below the horizon. The earthly years of Jesus were advancing toward the beginning, and were being drawn toward his birth in fullness.

Easter is a birth, but also a mystery of death, a unique mystery of birth and death. The earthly existence of Jesus already presented that double aspect. Jesus entered the world, both as Son of God in the holiness of the Spirit (cf. Lk 1:35) and as servant destined to death on the cross, "who, though he was in the form of God, did not regard equality with God as something to be exploited, but emptied himself, taking the form of a slave" (Phil 2:6–7). But he lived the condition of a slave in obedience, therefore, in submission to the Father, "When Christ came into the world, he said: ... 'See God, I have come to do your will'" (Heb 10:5–7). His descent into the depths under the conditions of a slave—he "became obedient to the point of death, even death on a cross" (Phil 2:8)—was also an ascent toward the glory of the Father. Jesus consented to do his Father's will and his humility led to glory. In this dramatic descent Saint John sees an exaltation, a lifting up from the earth (cf. Jn 12:32).

One can even dare to say that in this twofold movement that occurred simultaneously, it was the ascent, or the glorification, that was first. In some way it preceded the descent into slavery for it was the work of God as Father, whose act of begetting was the beginning of the mystery of Jesus. The entire action of the Father toward the Son found expression in the Resurrection, which was the divine begetting of Christ in his filial fullness.

Christ's death was submissive and transcendent. It was his passage from this world to the Father. It was all at once salvific on the part of the Father who, through life and death, begot Jesus and led him to obey, to do his will, and to die toward him. God drew Jesus into his bosom and had him born by dying toward the Father. Christ's death derives its meaning through the act of glorification, that is, the action of the Father through which Christ became Son. This is of prime importance. For theology it must be the steppingstone for reflection.

Christian faith has never lagged in placing Christ at the origins of the world. He is the Christ of glory in whom God makes the divine fullness to dwell.[12] John declared, "He was in the beginning....All things came into being through him" (Jn 1:2–3). But was he Christ, Man/Son of God, or "son" considered apart from the mystery of the Incarnation? One can debate the issue. In any case, it was from the mouth of Jesus, as the Gospel of John presents him, that one hears so often the phrase "I Am."

"Before Abraham was, I AM" (Jn 8:58). It was Christ whose day "Abraham...rejoiced that he would see...he saw it and was glad" (Jn 8:56). It is Christ who, in Revelation 19:13, bears the name Word of God, and who is the prince of all creation,[13] the Alpha and Omega of the divine works.[14] It was of him that Paul declared: "For us there is... one Lord, Jesus Christ, through whom are all things and through whom we exist" (1 Cor 8:6). It was of this Christ, who is the visible image of God, that Paul said yet again: "All things have been created through him and for him. He himself is before all things, and in him all things hold together" (Col 1:16–17).

To affirm the cosmic primacy of the Christ of glory, or to say that he is before all things and in him all things hold together, does not contradict the fact that Jesus lived in a particular period of history, that is, at the time of the emperors Augustus and Tiberius. For it is Jesus in his glory, in whom "the whole fullness of deity dwells bodily" (Col 2:9). If the fullness of being, life, and grace dwells in him, then anyone who shares that being, life, and grace depends on him and comes from him. Therefore, it is true that the Christ of glory was at the beginning of everything.[15]

These preliminary considerations have a certain usefulness. They show the importance of the Resurrection over against theologies that formerly held sway (and indeed are not entirely out of sight). Such theologies make the entire weight of redemption reside in only the passion of Christ. These considerations, however, show that Christ's death finds its salvific truth only in relationship to his exaltation.

Moreover, it appears that Christ Jesus attained salvation not only in an act that took place long ago, but glorified through his death he became salvation *in person* for all times, "having been made perfect [was glorified], he became the source of eternal salvation" (Heb 5:9) for all who enter into communion with him.

Because Christ, glorified in death, is salvation *in person*, we are invited to reconsider the notion that Christ paid a price to repair sin, and that the merits he thus acquired are applied to humans. Rather, we can now speak of Jesus in his filial relationship with God the Father, and of his entrance into total communion with the Father. Instead of applying the merits of Christ, we will speak of communion with him in his Passover through which he became salvation. Therefore, our image of God will be personal and not juridical as in other theologies that have prevailed for so long.

This does not merely suggest a new mode of thinking about the process of salvation, it also offers a point of departure for theological reflection. In the so-called juridical theologies, reparation of sin constituted the point of departure and ended with the death of Jesus. But the true point of departure is the mystery of the Resurrection—and that is its end, as well. Everything began in that mystery, for the Resurrection was the work of the Father. Here, the paternity of God becomes the beginning of everything. The resurrection was an act of love, an act of eternally begetting the Son according to the fullness of the Holy Spirit. That love is infinite and gratuitous. Absolutely gratuitous, it supersedes any notion of repairing sin or of satisfying justice. That infinite love was motivated only by itself, "God so loved the world that he gave his only Son" (Jn 3:16). "In Christ, God was reconciling the world to himself, not counting their trespasses" (2 Cor 5:19). To save sinful humans, with whom he was in solidarity, Jesus had nothing to give to his Father except what he already had. In his death on behalf of humans he opened himself up to the infinite love of the Father who begot his Son in the Holy Spirit. It is thus that he "takes away the sin of the world" (Jn 1:29).

These preliminary considerations and the conclusions drawn from them may appear hazy and hasty. In the following chapters, I will confirm them and make them more precise.

8

Chapter Two

LORD-MESSIAH, SON OF GOD

J esus is risen! That cry on the first day was an explosion of joy, but also a profession of faith. The disciples proclaimed that Jesus is the Messiah, "Therefore let the entire house of Israel know with certainty that God has made him both Lord and Messiah, this Jesus whom you crucified" (Acts 2:36).

THE MESSIAH-LORD

In raising Jesus from the dead, God enthroned him in messianic lordship. The disciples had begun to believe in Jesus' messiahship prior to his death. Struck by his authority, they asked themselves, "Is this not the Messiah?"[16] Peter had declared that he was (cf. Mk 8:29). But Peter was still unaware of the heavenly character of the messianic anointing (cf. Mk 8:31–33). On the day of his entrance into Jerusalem, Jesus claimed for the first time the title of Lord, "Untie it [the colt] and bring it. If anyone says to you, 'Why are you doing this?' just say this, 'The Lord needs it'" (Mk 11:2–3). God himself prepared the honors of that day,[17] anticipating by a week the entrance into messianic glory. But that victory was modest in keeping with the prophecy, "Tell the daughter of Zion, / 'Look, your king is coming to you, / humble and mounted on a donkey'" (Mt 21:5).[18] The Messiah was humble. The supreme anointing would be given to him in death, "We proclaim Christ [Messiah] crucified" (1 Cor 1:23).

In Scripture, "Lord" is the title for God in his universal power. The Jews also conferred it on God's representative on earth, the messiah-king. The royal psalm 110 had already received a messianic interpretation, "The Lord [God] said to my Lord [the king], 'Sit at my right hand'" (Mk 12:36). Through the Resurrection, Jesus was established in the messianic lordship (cf. Acts 2:36). From that moment on, the disciples gave him the title of Lord (cf. Rom 10:9). They gave this title to Jesus in the same sense as to God: to the one who became obedient even to death on the cross, God "gave him the name that is above every name...and every tongue should confess that Jesus Christ is Lord" (Phil 2:9, 11). Before the risen one Thomas confessed, "My Lord and my God!" (Jn 20:28). The earthly messianic hopes died in the death of Jesus. The title of Lord in its earthly and limited meaning was shattered. Instead, Jesus the Messiah reigns "seated at the right hand of the Power" (Mk 14:62) meaning, the exercise of universal power.[19] And he is the only Lord there is: "For us there is...one Lord, Jesus Christ, through whom are all things and through whom we exist" (1 Cor 8:6).

The entire power of God was, therefore, invested in the Father's act of raising Christ, and was communicated to the person Jesus. Saint Paul addressed what that power is: "If the Spirit of him who raised Jesus from among the dead dwells in you, he who raised Christ from the dead will give life to your mortal bodies also, through his Spirit that dwells in you" (Rom 8:11). Having been raised, Jesus was "established as Son of God in power according to the spirit of holiness" (Rom 1:4) [NAB]. The Holy Spirit is the all-powerfulness of God in action.

Elsewhere Paul is content to say that Jesus "lives by the power of God" (2 Cor 13:4)[20] But every reader of Scripture knows that the Holy Spirit is the power of God. Spirit and God are two interchangeable terms. From among so many texts let it suffice to cite the following: "The Holy Spirit will come upon you, and the power of the Most High will overshadow you" (Lk 1:35); "you will receive power when the Holy Spirit comes upon you (Acts 1:8); "our message of the gospel came to you not in word only, but also in power and in the Holy Spirit" (1 Thess 1:5). God carries out all work through the Holy Spirit. He creates through it, "When you send forth your spirit, they are created" (Ps 104:30).[21] Through the Spirit, God directs creation to its goal in the resurrection of the dead (cf. Rom 8:11). Through the Holy Spirit, God brought about the most powerful work of all, the Resurrection of Jesus.

Paul says yet again: "Christ was raised…by the glory of the Father" (Rom 6:4). Glory and power are connected realities.[22] Glory is the splendor of God in his astonishing works. It is the visible dimension of God's all-powerful holiness, "Holy, holy, holy is the LORD of hosts; / the whole earth is full of his glory" (Isa 6:3). Before the glory of God, humans are overawed. Examples from Scripture include: "In the morning you shall see the glory of the Lord" (Ex 16:7); "if you believed you would see the glory of God" (Jn 11:40), and the "glorious power" about which Colossians 1:11 speaks. The Spirit is the holiness of God in the splendor of his manifestations. Isaiah 63:10–14 outlines a comparison between the Holy Spirit and the dense, luminous cloud called "the glory of God," which was a sign of the all-powerful presence of the holy God. The New Testament also identifies the Spirit with glory, "the Spirit of glory which is the Spirit of God" (1 Pt 4:14).[23]

These three affirmations come together: raised by the Spirit, brought to life by the power, and raised by the glory. One day the faithful themselves will also rise by the Spirit, transformed in glory and power, thus becoming "a spiritual body" (1 Cor 15:44).

The power at work in the Resurrection of Jesus is infinite. The author of the Epistle to the Ephesians exhausts the limitation of words in describing it: "The immeasurable greatness of his power...God put this power to worked in Christ when he raised him from the dead" (Eph 1:19–20).[24] The omnipotence of the last day is fully displayed in the glorification of Jesus. According to Philippians, "the power of his resurrection" (3:10) is the very same power that will awaken all the dead. The triumph of the last day when "every knee should bend...and every tongue should confess that Jesus Christ is Lord" (Phil 2:10–11) is the response to obedience unto death. It is the impact that the power of the Resurrection has on the world. Jesus was taken over by the Holy Spirit to the point of becoming a life-giving spirit. He was taken over by the power (who is the Spirit), to the point of becoming the omnipotent Lord. And he was taken over by the glory (who is the Spirit), to the point of becoming "the Lord of glory" (1 Cor 2:8).

The power of God knows no limits, but apparently the greatest work of all was the Resurrection of Jesus. "The power" was conferred there in unlimited splendor, "the whole fullness of the deity dwells bodily" in the Christ of glory (Col 2:9). Thus, the risen Jesus is an unfathomable mystery. The Holy Spirit, who is the depth of God, has involved Jesus in this depth, has spiritualized him, and has divinized his humanity to become the very presence of God (cf. 1 Cor 15:45).[25] The Incarnation, which began at the moment of his earthly conception through the power of the Holy Spirit and was a reality from that moment, was fully displayed through his death (cf. Lk 1:35).

One should not be mistaken about the nature of the power that this Lord has at his disposal. It is of another order, contrary even to the total power a person in this world has at his or her disposal, "we proclaim Christ crucified...the power of God" (1 Cor 1:23–24). "Christ" is a title of glory, yet the Lord of glory was crucified. The conquering lion, lauded in triumphal hymns, is an immolated lamb (cf. Rev 5:5–6). Given in obedience unto death, his power cannot claim human greatness. The Spirit of the Resurrection is love (cf. Rom 5:5). True love is humble, and infinite love possesses a disconcerting humility. The self-emptying (*kenosis*) at the Incarnation was not rendered void by death, it was glorified (cf. Phil 2:6). The name that is above every other name has not been won by Jesus in victory. It has been bestowed[26] by God, given because of Christ's obedience, and humbly received. Jesus let himself be divinely begotten in death—his lordship is relational "to the glory of God the Father" (Phil 2:11).

THE SON

"Lord" is a title of function. But the word "son" expresses a relationship. To affirm his identity, Jesus spoke of himself as the son, "no one knows the Father except the Son" (Mt 11:27). God's truth resides in his fatherhood. "I made your name known to them" (Jn 17:26), for Jesus, God's name is "Father" because Jesus' truth resides in his filial relationship to the Father.

The paschal mystery is the summit of that divine relationship. In Romans, Paul distinguishes two phases in Jesus' existence. One coincides with the history of Israel, the other is of a universal and eschatological order, "the gospel about his Son, descended from David according to the flesh, but established as Son of God in power according to the Spirit of holiness through resurrection of the dead" (Rom 1:3–4) [NAB]. He was *established* as Son of God, therefore, he must have become such in some way. This does not mean that he was not son before and was subsequently adopted. The text makes the point, "established as Son of God *in power.*"[27] He had already been Son of God on earth, but he was so in his human weakness. The divine relationship, real from the moment of his conception, is evident in the beginning of the passage quoted above: "The gospel about *his Son,* descended from David according to the flesh...." It preceded the change in Jesus. The father/son relationship was present from the beginning. Nonetheless the change was real, "established"—and not only revealed—as Son of God. The resurrection established Jesus in the glorious, all-powerful truth of his sonship.

According to Acts of the Apostles, it was a divine begetting, (cf. Acts 13:33).[28] God's action of raising Jesus was paternal—it begot. Jesus was born and rose as Son of God.

Psalm 2 celebrates the enthronement of a king. In the theocratic nation of Israel, God consecrated this king by adopting him as a son. God had promised to David's descendant: "I will establish the throne of his kingdom forever. I will be a father to him, and he shall be a son to me" (2 Sam 7:13–14).[29] The titles "messiah-king" and "Son of God" could be used as synonyms. Jesus was first recognized as Son of God in a messianic sense. But he himself sought to show that the Messiah is not the Lord as a simple son of David (cf. Mk 12:35–37). He was Son of God in another way. He called upon God when he cried out, "Abba!" He gave God this name showing childlike intimacy and tenderness that no Jew ever gave to God. Christian faith has also understood Psalm 2 as indicating a transcendent filiation, "For to which of the angels did God ever say: 'You are my Son; today I have begotten you?'" (Heb 1:5; 5:5).

The act of raising Jesus was truly a begetting. A person who dies is no longer anything unless God takes hold of that person at the moment of death and reclaims him or her by drawing him or her unto himself. Jesus accepted death. He agreed to no longer exist except in God to whom he abandoned himself. In

Jesus' emptiness, God welcomed him as a son. Jesus was received by God, and begotten in the divine fullness of the Father dwelling within him bodily (cf. Col 2:9). Raised in death, Jesus now exists only through the Father, fully, divinely begotten.

In the act of begetting Jesus, God thus revealed Jesus as Son. The filial mystery is radiant. The word "Son" was glorified, made full of light, and pronounced by God in the Christophanies, in baptism, and on the mount of the transfiguration. Jesus pronounced it rejoicing in the Holy Spirit (cf. Lk 10:21–22). In Paul, it glows with the glory of the last day,[30] a glory that converted the apostle "when God...was pleased to reveal his Son" to him (Gal 1:15–16). Saint John saw "his glory, the glory as of a father's only son" (Jn 1:14).

At that point, Jesus became fully what he already was from his origin: the Son, born of God in the Holy Spirit (cf. Lk 1:35). His humanity was assumed into the eternal moment of his divine birth, "this day I beget you." After his resurrection, Jesus no longer lived as he was, but he was eternalized in that instant when the Father begot him in the Holy Spirit. Nothing further can happen to him. Nothing can be added to the fullness of divinity dwelling in him or to the unlimited power of the Resurrection (cf. Col 2:9). Jesus' Resurrection is that of the dead. It is the eschatological mystery.[31]

For Jesus, that ultimate mystery was the absolute beginning. His fundamental origin resided in the Father's act of begetting him. The disciples had first recognized him as the Messiah-Son of God, the descendant of David. Later, they understood that he was the only Son. However, the messianic character is second, following from his loving obedient relationship with the Father. In the beginning of this chapter, we raised the question of Christ's lordship. But it was to the Son that lordship was given (cf. Heb 1:5–8). It can be seen that, if he is savior, he is so precisely as Son in solidarity with humanity. As such, he is the mediator for creation.[32] According to Hebrews 5:5, he is the true high-priest because he is the Son. The mystery of Jesus is in his sonship. For him, everything began when he was begotten by the Father.

In raising Jesus, God actualized his paternity and by doing so, revealed it to the world. God revealed himself even more by this act than he had in word. The statement, "whoever has seen me has seen the Father" (Jn 14:9), is now verified with full brilliance. From that moment we know that God is the infinite Father of a Son whom he begot in the Holy Spirit. God's name is Father, "for us there is one God, the Father" (1 Cor 8:6). The faithful can say, "Blessed be the God and Father of our Lord Jesus Christ!…he has given us a new birth…through the resurrection of Jesus Christ" (1 Pet 1:3).[33] In his Passover, Jesus was the burning bush of the ultimate revelation. And God became among us creatures what truly is his nature: a Father who infinitely begets a Son.

SON OF GOD IN THE HOLY SPIRIT

It is through the Holy Spirit that God raised Jesus. That truth is essential. Paul says this again in Romans when he speaks of "the Spirit of him who raised Jesus from the dead" and who "will give life to our mortal bodies also through his Spirit" (Rom 8:11). He affirmed it when he attributed the resurrection to power in 2 Corinthians 13:4, for the Spirit is that power, and when he attributed it to the glory of God in Romans 6:4, for the Holy Spirit is the divine glory (cf. 1 Pet 4:14). In his resurrection, Jesus was taken over by "the power" to the point of becoming Lord (cf. Phil 2:9–11) and was taken over by God's glory to the point of becoming the Lord of glory (cf. 1 Cor 2:8). Jesus was transformed in the Holy Spirit to the point of himself becoming a life-giving spirit (cf. 1 Cor 15:45).

16

In the world today God is present as the Holy Spirit. God is "the spirit of holiness" (Rom 1:4). Such holiness in Scripture means divine transcendence. The Holy Spirit is "the power of the Most High" (Lk 1:35), a power that is God's alone. The Spirit is the reality of God from on high who must come down to earth in order to communicate God to us. That Spirit came upon Mary (cf. Lk 1:35). It also came down upon Jesus in the form of a dove (cf. Mt 3:16), and it came from heaven like a strong driving wind (cf. Acts 2:2). Because Jesus was conceived of the Spirit, he is "holy" (Lk 1:35), and "from above" (Jn 8:23), that is to say, he is of the divine order—he is "the Holy One of God" (Jn 6:69). In his glory, having become a life-giving spirit, Jesus was fully sanctified (cf. Jn 17:19), or as Saint Ambrose put it, he was "formerly man according to the flesh, now fully God."[34] Having been raised, Jesus is Man/God in the fullest sense of that paradox. Paul speaks of the Spirit of Christ (cf. Rom 8:9), and of the Spirit of the Son (cf. Gal 4:6). He thus affirmed the divinity of Jesus, because obviously the Spirit of God is proper only to God. It would be absurd to refer to the Spirit of Christ if Christ were not God.

But it is not enough to call Jesus the Man/God. His complete identity is Man/Son of God, where he is Son of God through the Holy Spirit. The paschal mystery is filial. It was carried out in the Spirit of the Son through whom Jesus was offered to the Father (cf. Heb 9:14) and through whom he was raised by the Father (cf. Rom 8:11).

The mystery that culminated on Easter was at work from Jesus' birth. According to Augustine, during Jesus' life on earth "everything was at the service of the resurrection."[35] Two gospels recount Jesus' earthly birth and convey its divinely filial meaning. Matthew sets up the genealogy and lists its many generations, "so and so begot so and so, who begot so and so, who, etc." The verb "to beget" is always in the active tense, but toward the end a sudden change, a break occurs. From then on the verb is in the passive tense, "Jacob begot Joseph, the husband of Mary, of whom Jesus *was begotten*" (Mt 1:16) [Douay-Rheims]. The verb in the passive tense designates the divine author of the begetting.[36] The place of Jesus in the genealogy is assured by Joseph, the husband of Mary, but God himself is the father of the child. His birth, though placed at the end, goes back prior to his distant ancestor, Abraham, who is first on the list. In John's gospel, Jesus put it this way: "Before Abraham was, I am" (Jn 8:58). While the roles of the men and of God are expressed by the verb "to beget," the role of the women is described by the preposition "of." Jesus was begotten by God of Mary, but not of her alone—of the Holy Spirit and of Mary (cf. Mt 1:18–20). Thus a person had been begotten who was the Son of God.

In the infancy narrative of Luke, the Holy Spirit is named three times: first under its proper name, then by "the power" which is a synonym for the Spirit, and finally by an overshadowing that Scripture calls "the glory of God." Glory is also a synonym for the Holy Spirit. "The Holy Spirit will come upon you, and the power of the Most High will overshadow you. Therefore the child to be born will be called holy, the Son of God" (Lk 1:35). The child will be the Holy One, Son of God, because he is born of the Spirit. The Holy Spirit does not play the role of a husband with a wife. No, the child would be the Son, not of the Spirit, but of God the Father. The Spirit is merely the power in whom God begets.

The two accounts of Jesus's birth are echoes reverberating ahead of Christ's much more prodigious paschal birth. Even in the paschal birth, as in the scriptural genealogy, continuity was assured, "…Jesus of Nazareth, who was crucified. He has been raised" (Mk 16:6). However, the break that time was much more profound than in the virginal conception, for it was through death that Jesus was "established as Son of God in power according to the spirit of holiness" (Rom 1:4) [NAB]. From the beginning Jesus was the Son in the Spirit. After his resurrection he is Son in glorious fullness. He is forever the Nazarean, born of Mary. But he exists only through his Father-Creator who begot and created him in the Holy Spirit. This is a mysterious action that, for the man Jesus, is an act both of begetting and of creation.

The infancy narratives, written in the light of Easter, cast light on this paschal mystery. We already knew that the Resurrection of Jesus was the divine begetting of the Son by the power of the Holy Spirit. The infancy accounts provide a confirmation of that fact. It was in the Holy Spirit that God begot his Son into this world.

The Holy Spirit continued to be the inseparable companion of Jesus during his ministry.[37] John the Baptist recognized Jesus as the Son of God, because the Spirit remained on him (cf. Jn 1:32–34). On the mountain of the transfiguration, the glory of God took hold of Jesus and the disciples in its luminous darkness. The voice of God proclaimed, "This is my Son, the Beloved" (Mt 17:5). Wasn't that glorious cloud a symbol of the Spirit?

Neither Jesus nor the Spirit are fully known in their profound truth apart from their mutual relationship. It is the action of the Spirit that conferred on Jesus his filial identity.[38] The Holy Spirit is recognized in ultimate truth by its involvement in the filial mystery of Jesus. We knew from the Hebrew Scriptures that the Holy Spirit is the power by whom God carries out all his works. Until the Resurrection we did not know that the Spirit is the power behind the divine begetting. Inseparable, the Spirit and Jesus reveal each other.

This twofold revelation came to its fullness in the Resurrection. But to reach that summit, Jesus had to travel a long road in the power of the Holy Spirit.

Chapter Three

THE BEGETTING OF THE SON IN HISTORY

T he human person on earth is history; it is the nature of humans to become. It was the same for Jesus in his destiny as Man/Son of God. In the Trinitarian mystery the Father begot the Son in instantaneous fullness. Yet God's eternity is dynamic. All of eternity is an infinite moment of the Father begetting the Son. Jesus was the Son from his origin. Yet the Father continued to beget him throughout his life of loving obedient consent until the begetting became complete through his death and resurrection.[39]

Jesus defined himself as "the one whom the Father has sanctified" (Jn 10:36). Before his passion he declared, "Now I sanctify myself" (Jn 17:19). Hence, the sanctification had not yet been total. Glory, a characteristic of filiation, was still only dimly visible (cf. Jn 1:14). Jesus asked for it as if it were absent, "Father, the hour has come. Glorify your son" (Jn 17:1). To be the Son is to be in the bosom of the Father (cf. Jn 1:18), and one with him (cf. Jn 10:30). At that time Jesus still had to go to the Father (cf. Jn 14:12). He had to ascend (cf. Jn 6:62) to where he had his origin (cf. Jn 8:23). His mission was carried out by that process.

According to Paul, Jesus was first subjected to a condition of life that was not in keeping with the mystery of his relationship with the Father (cf. Phil 2:7). "Born of a woman, born under the law" (Gal 4:4), he belonged to a people who were like a child that has not yet inherited its father's property, in this case, those goods that are from the Spirit of filiation. In Jesus' own passage from life of a slave to life of a son, he brought that Spirit of filiation to his faithful ones, also (cf. Gal 4:1–6). His mission was carried out through a personal process of surrendering to the Father. He became the Good News *in person* when he attained his filial fullness, "We bring you the good news that what God promised...he has fulfilled by raising Jesus, as also it is written in the second psalm: 'You are my son; today I have begotten you'" (Acts 13:32–33).

The Epistle to the Hebrews speaks of this "becoming," of this "achievement,"[40] where Christ, although Son, learned obedience, was made perfect, and thus became the source of salvation for all (cf. Heb 5:8–9).

In consenting to the Father who begot him, Jesus became what he was from birth: the Son. It is like all of us who, though Christian by baptism, must continually grow in being Christian until the time of our death. Jesus let himself be filialized, "became obedient to the point of death—even death on a cross. Therefore, God also highly exalted him" (Phil 2:8–9).

It is the Father who led him toward fullness. Without the Father, the Son would not have known the way to it: "The Son can do nothing on his own, but only what he sees the Father doing; for whatever the Father does, the Son also does likewise" (Jn 5:19). The knowledge Jesus had was at the level of a son who must still become fully "the only Son, close to the Father's heart" (Jn 1:18).

A theological opinion has prevailed over the centuries that attributed the beatific vision to Jesus from the start of his earthly life. It held that as the Man-God, Jesus enjoyed unlimited knowledge proper to God and to heavenly bliss. In such a belief system, Jesus' salvific work was fulfilled through an act that had nothing to do with him personally. That is, he merely paid the debt incurred by someone else to the offended justice of God. This system did not consider that redemption had to be carried out *in the Redeemer*—that is, in his passage from this world to the Father, from the condition of slave to the full life of the Son. Jesus became the savior when salvation was fulfilled *in his person*, through communion with the Father that had not been complete in every regard before his death.

For Jesus ignorance did not seem incompatible with his filial dignity. For example, he acknowledged not knowing the date of the final day (cf. Mk 13:32). That affirmation of his relation to the Father was solemn. The Son was above human beings and even the angels, but the date of the end of time was reserved to the Father alone. Jesus knew that the heavenly reign would revert to him, but it was up to the Father to designate who would sit at his right and at his left (cf. Mk 10:40).

In Gethsemane, faced with the frightening fate that awaited him, he "prayed that, if it were possible, the hour might pass from him" (Mk 14:35). "…if it were possible"—he knew a great deal, but he did not know everything.

How could Jesus have been enjoying a heavenly vision, and at the same time feel "grieved even to death" (Mk 14:34), utterly desperate with sorrow?

The knowledge of the human Jesus was appropriate to his identity: it was as a lovingly obedient son. It was not an omniscient knowledge of the many realities and events in the world. Such knowledge was unique, proper to the Only One, not shareable with the human Jesus.[41] For the human Jesus, there was nothing more he could learn. His knowledge was of God in mystery, of God as a father. Jesus knew he was in a filial relationship with

God. It seems that Jesus never knew and could not have known God other than as his Father.[42] Otherwise he would not have known God as he truly is.

The divine filiation was relational. A personal relationship is a conscious one.[43] Even at the end of his life, Jesus called God by the name of confidence and intimacy that a child gives to its dad, Abba! No doubt this was the name that as a small child he gave to God who had been revealed in his heart. Throughout life, Jesus continued that habit and kept that attitude toward his beloved and gracious Father (cf. Jn 14:28).

Yet Jesus, already Son in communion with the Father, could still enter into a more intense communion. Likewise his filial awareness could intensify to the point of supreme transparency through death where communion with the Father became total.

Indeed, Jesus' knowledge increased while he was growing up. Not only did he learn to speak, to read, and to discover the geography of his country, but through his Father he became aware of his mission and of the means to accomplish it. That messianic awareness was inseparable from his filial awareness because his mission was to live as Son of God for the salvation of all until the fullness of the filial mystery appeared through the glory of his death.

The mission was, therefore, inscribed in his being as Man/Son of God. In this sense the messianic awareness in Jesus was as old as his filial awareness.

But at the same time, his messianic awareness was able to become more explicit and be enriched by new experiences. The gospel accounts lead us to think that Jesus did not always know far in advance the precise road he had to take. John, whose admiration for Jesus' wisdom is certainly great,[44] acknowledges that Jesus let himself be guided by his Father step by step. What he said and did, he received from the Father in proportion to the needs of the mission (cf. Jn 8:28): "The Father loves the Son and shows him all that he himself is doing, and he will show him greater works than these" (Jn 5:20). The Son advanced with his eyes fixed on the Father, the Father guided the hand of the Son through the Son's heart. God the Father loves his Son, Jesus loves the Father and does "as the Father has commanded me" (Jn 14:31). The Father, who constantly begets Jesus, begets him in all his activities[45] with the insights that he needs.

When Jesus came into the filial fullness and his awareness reached its highest intensity, the messianic awareness no longer involved any ignorance. All power in heaven and on earth was given to him. Asked by his disciples, he would no longer say that he knows neither the day nor the hour. They are the ones who are not to know it for the sake of their mission (cf. Acts 1:6–7).

The opinion that long held sway that Jesus possessed a universal and beatific knowledge was not completely erroneous. The error was in the nature of the knowledge and the vision. It was said, "The ultimate and perfect beatitude can only be in the vision of the divine essence…the very essence of the first cause."[46] But the ultimate beatitude is actually the experiential knowledge of God in his mystery and his paternity.[47]

For Jesus, eternal happiness is to be the Begotten of the Father, and to be aware of it. From the time he came to earth, he possessed this knowledge and the corresponding happiness. But it was adapted to his earthly condition. To know himself as the Son was happiness for Jesus. It gave his life meaning, provided assurance, and sometimes made him rejoice (cf. Lk 10:21). The seed of eternal knowledge and the vision were already there. But filial awareness did not preclude ignorance of the events and realities of the world. And far from excluding suffering, it increased it on that day when God, while still his Father, appeared so distant (cf. Mk 15:34).

The Father begot Jesus in the Spirit, who is love. He begot him by loving him. Relations of love are established in freedom —Jesus had to let himself be begotten. Jesus had to be obediently receptive to whatever the Father, who takes the initiative, gave him. Obviously, a donor cannot give to someone who refuses to receive the gift. In biblical language such receptivity is called obedience, which is the main filial virtue. Jesus was the preeminently free person. He was free from the traditions of the scribes and Pharisees. He opposed the image that they formed of God. Jesus was free to rebel against the high priests who abused their authority over the temple. He was free even from himself in total self-renunciation. But to God he lived in absolute submission.

That submission was his source of liberty, even under the limitations that his earthly existence imposed on him. He had parents to whom he owed obedience, but he broke free of those bonds for three days to "be in his Father's house" (cf. Lk 2:49–51). He was neither husband nor father of a family—he was uniquely the only Son. With faith in his Father, he raised himself above the constraints of physical laws and worked miracles. His submission to God found expression in acts of freedom.

But his obedience had not yet reached its high point: "He became obedient to the point of death" (Phil 2:8). He became. It is not that he ever disobeyed, but an earthly human is incapable of total union with God's will, or of any eternal act. Having obeyed God today, we must begin again tomorrow. Sufferings racked Jesus in making his required eternal consent. A Christian who lives his or her trials in faith and charity opens himself or herself to God to a depth unknown before. Likewise Christ "learned obedience through what he suffered" and was made perfect (Heb 5:8–9). Thus the passion of Jesus was not punishment inflicted on an Innocent One whom God substituted for sinners.[48]

26

The disobedient ancestor was replaced by the new Adam "who became obedient to the point of death" (cf. Rom 5:12–18). Redemption is a work of obedience in mutual love: "For this reason the Father loves me, because I lay down my life in order to take it up again....I have received this command from my Father" (Jn 10:17–18).

Jesus was a man of deep prayer. The Father does not have to pray, just as he does not have to obey. He is the source, and does not need anything that he does not already possess. Prayer is an attribute of the Son. All prayer is basically an invocation of the Father: "When you pray, say: Father!" (Lk 11:2). A person praying recognizes the fatherhood of God, opens himself or herself up to it, and lets himself or herself be begotten. The child of God is progressively being created when a person enters into prayer.

Jesus prayed a great deal. He spoke of an abundance of the heart when he recommended prayer without ceasing (cf. Lk 18:1). He laid himself open to his Father, allowing God to act as a Father. He prayed in the Holy Spirit (cf. Lk 10:21). He said "Abba!" just as the disciples would do when moved by the Spirit.[49] The Spirit is the divine power in whom God begets the Son. By praying, Jesus became the Son that he was: "While he was praying, the appearance of his face changed" (Lk 9:29). It became truly the face of one about whom God proclaimed: "This is my Son" (Lk 9:35).

Jesus "went up on the mountain to pray" (Lk 9:28). To reunite with God, one must go up, for God is the Holy One, the Transcendent One. Jesus had yet to go up. Prayer is defined as a "lifting up of the spirit to God."[50] In his death Jesus lifts himself "up from the earth" (Jn 12:32) not only in his spirit but also by his very being. He became prayer, the prayer of all humanity in his infinite consent to the fatherhood of God. God, who raised Jesus, hears Jesus in himself as well as for humanity: "He died for all...him who was raised for them" (2 Cor 5:15).

The fact that Jesus prayed a great deal shows that his filial mystery knew that it had to develop. He was already one with the Father (cf. Jn 10:30), yet Jesus still had to go to him (cf. Jn 14:28). As long as Jesus lived on earth, one part of him was at the threshold of the Father's house. Similar to the high priest who once a year entered the sanctuary made of human hands, Jesus entered the temple not made by human hands, through the veil of his flesh, "thus obtaining eternal redemption" (Heb 9:12).[51] He entered into communion. His death was a liturgy of communion.

The paschal hour was announced in the great prayers of Jesus. According to Luke, Jesus prayed from the moment of his baptism which prefigured the paschal mystery. He prayed on the mountain where the disciple saw "Moses and Elijah talking to him" of the exodus he would accomplish in Jerusalem (cf. Lk 9:29–30). He prayed in Gethsemane—a prelude to his death. His last prayer according to Luke was an act of obedient commitment into the hands of the Father (cf. Lk 23:46). According to the evangelist, that was the whole meaning of Jesus' death. His final public act linked up with his first one where, as a twelve-year-old boy, he said he needed to "be in my Father's house" (Lk 2:49). And we know the Father heard Jesus' prayer when he said: "You are my Son; today I have begotten you" (Acts 13:33; Heb 5:5).

DEATH, THE FILIAL MYSTERY

What happened in the death of Jesus? There were no witnesses who can describe it exactly. The spectators at Calvary were hidden from the real drama by a curtain of human flesh. They saw a man who was dying, then a man who was dead. The Father alone witnessed the death of the Son. But he unveiled its mystery by raising Jesus: in his death Jesus was divinely born.

But the Father was not just a simple witness—he was the primary actor. In saying, "He who did not withhold his own Son" (Rom 8:32), Saint Paul recalls Abraham who was ready to sacrifice Isaac.[52] "The chief priests and leaders handed him over" (Lk 24:20); Pilate "handed him over" (Mt 27:26). The Father also "gave him up for all of us" (Rom 8:32). Jesus knew himself to be given up by the Father: "This is my body, which is given for you" (Lk 22:19). The verb in the passive tense attributes the action to God.[53] When Jesus insisted that "the Son of Man must undergo great suffering" (Mk 8:31), he stated that his destiny was written in "the definite plan" of the Father (cf. Acts 2:23). *But God handed him over differently.* The others handed him over in order to kill him, to dismiss him from Israel and from history. The Father handed him over in order to beget him and to place him at the center of everything. Peter thus distinguished God's role from the others: "You killed the Author of Life, whom God raised from the dead"(Acts 4:15).[54] God did not prevent human beings from killing Jesus,[55] but he did not intend his death to end as the others did. Being Father, God willed to beget Jesus through his death.

Therefore, the death of Jesus, the Son, was necessary. The phrase "he must" that is so insistent and often repeated[56] expresses the necessity which was inscribed in the divine plan. Why was it necessary? To expiate the sins of human beings? That will be taken up in the next chapter. The first reason was Jesus, in his relationship with the Father, where the mission of salvation is carried out: "Was it not necessary that the Messiah should suffer these things and then enter into his glory?" (Lk 24:26). Jesus' painful death was necessary to bring about his glorious birth.

To be born "Son of God with power" (Rom 1:4), it was necessary for him to die "weakened by the flesh…in the likeness of sinful flesh" (Rom 8:3). What is good for human beings is good for their head (cf. Heb 2:10): "Flesh and blood cannot inherit the kingdom of God" (1 Cor 15:50).[57]

It was necessary to go to a place beyond this world in order to receive "the whole fullness of deity" (Col 2:9). That was where the Father, the one who begets, could receive him. To be Son is to be received by the Father. An infinite reception must correspond to the infinite begetting. The two infinites were joined together in the death and the resurrection. Jesus let himself be emptied, but he did so by handing himself over to the One who begets him. From then on he lives only by the One who raised him.

By receiving the fullness of God, Jesus could then contain in his own person all human beings. He had to die "to gather into one the dispersed children of God" (Jn 11:52), to gather them by incorporating them into himself. Because of the infiniteness of Christ's passion, the words can be verified: "On that day you will know that...you [are] in me" (Jn 14:20). Those words addressed to the disciples has universal importance, because it means that all human beings are called to be saved "in Christ...who became...redemption" (1 Cor 1:30). His death had to be infinite.

In a theology that considers the death of Jesus as the entrance into a glorious filial communion, one may sometimes seek to tone down the anguish of the passion. According to certain theologies, Jesus died separated from the Father, abandoned, crushed under the weight of sins and of the divine justice unleashed against them. But what could be more excruciating for a person than to be obliged to open oneself to God's infiniteness? Or to measure up to God's holiness and accept into oneself all of sinful humanity? Or to include humanity in one's own holiness? Certainly, the weight of human sins is enormous. But none of those sins, not even in their totality, is infinite as much as the glory of the Resurrection is infinite. Who could gather the ocean in the hollow of one's hand? Still more disproportionate was the relation between the earthly humanity of Jesus and the divine fullness that was going to "dwell bodily" in him (cf. Col 2:9). What wounding, what racking, and what distension did he not have to undergo? "He learned obedience through what he suffered, and [was] made perfect" (Heb 5:8–9). In Jesus' passion there was produced the "eternal weight of glory" (2 Cor 4:17) of the Resurrection. That reveals that the meaning of Jesus' death is its measure, which is infinite. In the holiness of God that Jesus received—which is greater than all sins—Jesus can enjoin all humanity, enveloping us in his infinite holiness.

Jesus was able to die an infinite death because he bore within himself the principle of infinite reception: he was the eternal Son incarnating himself even to the point of human death. In that instant he was assumed with all his humanity into the infinite receptivity of divine filiation. The Father accomplished what the Trinitarian mystery is all about: the Father begot the Son, granting him the gift that allows Jesus to be infinitely begotten. The emptying of the Son unto death—the *kenosis* of which Philippians 2:6 speaks—is the radical effect of the Son being begotten into the world. The executioners killed him, but his death in his infinite status as Son, that is, his dying unto the Father, was the supreme gift granted by the Father to the Son who was begotten into the world.

From the origins of Jesus, his emptied existence was rich with a secret glory, the glory of obedience, of filiality. Under the ashes the fire smoldered, setting everything ablaze when the emptying became total. The *kenosis*, that self-emptying, made Jesus totally receptive. Together with the resurrection it constitutes a unique mystery that will never pass away.[58]

AN ETERNAL BIRTH IN DEATH

Begotten in death, Jesus lives there, where he was eternally begotten. His loving obedient life and death form the unique paschal mystery. In rising, Jesus left the tomb, but he did not exit the mystery of his death. He kept the wounds of his passion, like the one on his side where Thomas could put his hand. Those wounds were mortal. Up to the last day (cf. Rev 1:7), humans "will look on the one whom they have pierced" (Jn 19:37). Standing in glory, Jesus is the conquering lion and the slaughtered lamb (cf. Rev 5:5–6). The sprinkled blood that expiates sins and sanctifies sinners forms part of an eternal liturgy.[59] The faithful always have entrance into "the sanctuary...by the new and living way that he opened for us through the curtain (that is, through his flesh)" (Heb 10:19–20). According to John 17:1–2, Jesus asked to be glorified in the presence of the Father in order to give eternal life to those who belonged to him. In John 12:32, he likewise announced that he would draw all people to himself when he was lifted up from the earth to heaven. However, the evangelist noted that his exaltation above the earth would be accomplished by the cross. The same movement, therefore, has its conclusion in death and in glory. The cross is the throne of eternal glory.

When men and women encounter Christ today, it is always in his death as he is being raised up. Through baptism, we become one body with him, and we die and rise together with him (cf. 1 Cor 12:13).[60] When he gives himself to us, it is as a body handed over and blood poured out.[61]

The begetting of Jesus demanded that he remain in the mystery of his death, in his dying toward the Father, and in the Father receiving him. By glorifying him, the Father did not snatch away his glory as Man/Son of God. The Resurrection does not void his obedience to the point of death, or his gift of self whereby Jesus rejoined his Father, who is love. If the Risen One had continued to live beyond death as he was before his death, he could not be linked to other human beings who are still doomed to die. He would not be the head of the earthly Church composed of mortal humans because then no one could die "with" him (cf. 2 Tim 2:11), or share in *his* resurrection (cf. Phil 3:10). Rather, his death is communion with the Father and with humankind. His death was not an end—it is eternal.

To rise while remaining in death can appear contradictory. However, reason easily admits the paradox when dealing with death as a filial mystery. According to Saint John, Jesus' death is the summit of his ascent to the Father. His glorifying encounter took place at that summit, not beyond it—hence in death. His glorification was an act of eternal fullness: eternal glorification holds Jesus in the death from which glory is inseparable. His glorification is eternal today. His death is also.

According to Luke 23:46, in his death Jesus commended himself into the hands of the Father. According to Hebrews 9:14, his death was Jesus offering himself to the Father. For any "giving" to take place, it is necessary that there be a corresponding gesture of acceptance. In giving himself, Jesus did not fall into a void—rather, he was received by the Father. These two gestures are connected to each other. The hands that receive him, glorify him. Eternal glorification holds Jesus in that moment when he placed himself in the hands of the Father.

Jesus merited salvation by his death. To merit is to receive a gift from God. Jesus was filled at the moment God received him, not afterward. The eternal fullness that fills him keeps him in a posture of receiving, and through it he continually merits redemption. He merits the salvation of the world eternally.[62]

The Incarnation became complete at the conclusion of his descent into the human condition, that is, in his death. The Son never left the lowly level of his Incarnation where the Father begot him as human.

Christ's redemptive death was not only a past act, it is eternal. Christ "became for us...redemption" (1 Cor 1:30). He is the redemption *in person*, the permanent crucible, recasting sinful humanity into "a new creation" (2 Cor 5:17).

The unity of Christ's death and resurrection is realized in the Holy Spirit. Jesus offers himself through an "eternal spirit" (Heb 9:14). He opened himself up as Son to the Father in the spirit of sonship (cf. Rom 8:15). The Father raised Jesus in the Holy Spirit (who is God's paternal power). In the Spirit, the Father begets; in the Spirit, the Son lets himself be begotten. Just as in the intimate mystery of God, the Spirit is one person in two others, and fuses them all into a unity, so the Spirit makes a unique mystery of Christ's death and resurrection. The Son died in the love of the Father (cf. Jn 14:31). The Father raised him by loving him. The Spirit is love and makes the death and resurrection a unique mystery of love. The Spirit thus assures the permanent reality of redemption, and reveals that Jesus remains always in the same death through which he is raised.

The paschal mystery is Trinitarian. The Son opened himself to the Father and let himself be begotten. The Father, from whom everything comes, enabled the Son to die in order to beget him in death. The unique Spirit of God is both paternal and filial. It is the power of both death and resurrection.

By emphasizing the importance of resurrection, the theology of paschal mystery does not lessen the importance of Christ's death in any way. But his death no longer appears as a single event of the past, and hence out of date. Rather, it is eternal. In Christ's death and in his resurrection, the Trinitarian mystery is imprinted on creation.

NOTE ON "THE THIRD DAY"

The unity of Christ's death and Resurrection as one sole mystery seems contradicted by this text: "Christ died for our sins in accordance with the scriptures; …he was buried; and that he was raised on the third day in accordance with the scriptures" (1 Cor 15:3–4). One could think that the unity of Christ's death and resurrection depends on a Gnostic type of thinking, that is, on speculation not rooted in history. Jesus, dead on the cross, was raised from the tomb, not from the cross. Theology must take that into account. The unity of his death and resurrection, however, is also based on Scripture. Therefore, the theological statement and the historical fact do not contradict each other.

In Hebrew to say "a little after," or "immediately after," one would say "the second day" or "the third day." Hosea writes: "For it is he who has torn, and he will heal us....After two days he will revive us; on the third day he will raise us up" (Hos 6:1–2). The prophet is not counting the days, but promises that after the disasters described salvation will not be long in coming. Other texts come to mind, such as 1 Corinthians 15:4: "The third day in accordance with the scriptures" (notice the plural). Indeed Scripture speaks of divine interventions that happen on the third day.[63] That formula had become the traditional way of recalling God's saving intervention. Jesus himself announced the rebuilding of the temple in three days (cf. Jn 2:19). One is also aware that at the time of Jesus, Hosea 6:1–2 was interpreted in terms of the eschatological catastrophe and the final resurrection of Israel.[64] Certainly, Christian faith considered the resurrection of Jesus as being a resurrection from the dead.[65] Yet this set of data suggests that "the third day" is not a precise indication of time. It means that God's act of salvation is not delayed, but also that his saving intervention is, no doubt, that of the end time. Who knows at what moment Jesus was raised? The fact that he appeared for the first time on Easter probably contributed to introducing the formula "the third day" into the community's preaching.

It remains that Jesus, dead on the cross, was raised from the tomb. Different solutions can be offered. For example, dead on the cross, his soul entered from there into glory. His body, laid in the tomb, was later assumed into the glory that coincided with his death.

Modern science can offer another explanation for it distinguishes "clinical death" and "absolute death," whose criterion we do not actually know. Absolute death can occur well after clinical death. Death was obviously verified on Calvary, yet real death could only occur in the tomb. In that case, nothing would stand in the way of death and resurrection occurring at the same time. According to one Jewish view at the time of Jesus, the soul of a person remained with the body for three days, only to leave when corruption set in.[66] Peter said: "He was not abandoned to Hades, nor did his flesh experience corruption" (Acts 2:31). Could that be an allusion to such a view, as in John 11:39? These hypotheses notwithstanding, perhaps the explanation is found in his infinite death, full of the Spirit in whom Jesus rose, and who is the only Spirit of death and resurrection. Christ's death was saturated with divine fullness. In Christ's death, the begetting of the Son into eternity and into time as we experience it in our world are joined together. Reason cannot capture a moment of eternity in time, or an incarnation of eternity into history, much less the Incarnation of God himself into humanity.

The theologically certain unity of the death and resurrection must not be denied simply because it poses a problem for reason. After all, the whole mystery in which the Father led Jesus to die completely toward him by begetting him in the fullness of the Holy Spirit is unfathomable.

Chapter Four

JESUS BECOME REDEMPTION

E verything that can be said is said about the paschal mystery whenever anyone affirms that, dead and raised, Jesus has fully become what he was from the beginning: the Son of God in the Holy Spirit. That is true, providing that one specifies: "And he died for all…and was raised for them" (2 Cor 5:15). In his paschal mystery Jesus is the savior, because it is *for us* that the Father begot him in the Spirit and Jesus allowed himself to be begotten.

JURIDICAL THEOLOGY

For a long time there has existed a theology of redemption significantly different from what is being described in this book. It might be called "juridical theology." In it the Resurrection of Jesus plays only a secondary role. This theology does not consider it important that Jesus, the Man/God, was "Son" in his relationship to the Father, and it totally by-passes the Holy Spirit in silence. Such juridical theology has held sovereign sway for centuries. It permeated minds and still leaves deep impressions. Examining that theology is useful to us not only for underlining its deficiencies but also for bringing out by contrast features of a theology of the paschal mystery.

Leaving aside the many nuances and corrections intended to mitigate its deficiencies, juridical theology is understood as follows. Humankind greatly sinned and divine justice was compelled to demand an adequate reparation, that is, an infinite reparation. No human being was capable of that—only the mystery of the Incarnation provided its possibility. Jesus, the Man/God, whose every action possessed infinite value, satisfied divine justice by his sufferings and death and gained for humans pardon and the right to eternal life. Redemption was not accomplished in the person of Jesus, or because of his relationship to God, but only by his sufferings and death. In this theology, we humans do not share in Christ's death by communion with him, but, rather, we share in it only through the application of its merits. That is to say, through faith we receive the effects won by his death.

Each of these two theologies—that of the paschal mystery and that of the juridical type—has its own image of God. In the paschal mystery type, God is a father whose preoccupation is the salvation of human beings. From the total generosity of his love, God begot the Son into the world for all humanity so that, instead of continuing to live as sinners, they may become his children. In juridical theology, on the other hand, God is first and foremost concerned about his own rights; and God pardons only after reparation of the offense has been accomplished.

The basic approach to thought is also different between these two: personal in one, juridical in the other. In paschal mystery theology we speak of communion, of salvation accomplished in Christ through his relationship to the Father, and of spreading salvation to the world by communion with Christ. Whereas juridical theology speaks of offended and repaired rights, of rights acquired by Christ in favor of humans, and of the application of those rights to us humans. The word communion is not even mentioned.

Since the time of the Reformation many theologians have given juridical theology a highly dramatic character. Jesus not only paid for sinful humanity, he was its substitute[67]—either by divine decree, or by taking on the flesh of sinful humanity. Having become like incarnated sin, he brought upon himself the wrath imposed by sin and descended into the hell of abandonment, even of rejection by God.[68] This tragic vision—where God is himself opposed to his Son: God against God—stirred up the eloquence of both Catholic and Protestant preachers.

In modern times some eminent theologians have again taken up this theory, seeking to clear it of juridical images by placing the painful separation between Father and Son in the very intimacy of the Trinity.[69] These theologians appeal especially to two Pauline texts: "He [God] made him [Christ] to be sin who knew no sin, so that in him we might become the righteousness of God" (2 Cor 5:21); and "Christ redeemed us from the curse of the law by becoming a curse for us" (Gal 3:13). The First Book of Peter (2:22–24) may also be added to these texts, "He committed no sin…He himself bore our sins in his body on the cross."

On further examination, however, it seems that the juridical theory does not find support in any of these texts.[70]

JESUS, SALVATION AND SAVIOR

According to the uncontested theologian on the justification of sinners, Saint Paul, salvation is not merely an act previously performed for them to which sinners can appeal. It is also a permanent reality in Christ with whom they can enter into communion: "He is the source of your life in Christ Jesus, who became for us wisdom from God, and righteousness and sanctification and redemption" (1 Cor 1:30). It is this Christ-salvation that God manifests to humans so that, through faith, we may find justification in him: "all have sinned and fall short of the glory of God; they are now justified by his grace as a gift, through the redemption that is in Christ Jesus, whom God put forward as a sacrifice of atonement by his blood, effective through faith" (Rom 3:23–25). Paul is alluding here to the ceremony over the propitiatory in the temple, that massive gold lid that covered the Ark of the Covenant. The high priest would sprinkle it with sacrificed blood on the annual feast of the Atonement. Israel was thus "expiated," that is, purified of its sins and consecrated to God.[71] "Covered with his own blood, from then on Jesus plays the role outlined of old for the propitiatory in the ceremony of expiation."[72] The Jewish propitiatory was enclosed in the Holy of Holies in the temple; but Jesus, in his immolation ("by his blood"), was exposed to the eyes of the world as the instrument of justification for all. In other words, he was the crucible placed in the midst of the world, into which all human beings are invited to enter through faith. Jesus is the redeemer because, through the death in which he was raised,[73] he became forever our redemption. He is the savior because he is salvation *in person* in the eternal paschal mystery.[74]

The frequent formulas "in Christ" and "Christ in us" attest to this. He is himself the salvation who, through communion, became the salvation of humankind: "Your life in Christ Jesus, who became for us…redemption" (1 Cor 1:30). The same is true for the phrase "with Christ" when it deals with sufferings, or with the death and resurrection shared with him.[75] We take part in the salvation realized in Christ:[76] "You were buried with him in baptism, you were also raised with him through faith" (Col 2:12). Jesus is "the last Adam [who] became a life-giving spirit" (1 Cor 15:45). He is the life-principle of a saved humanity. When anyone puts on Christ, he or she procures for him or herself the salvation of death and resurrection that is Christ in person.

Redemption is not reduced, therefore, to a simple act that occurred long ago. It is realized in Christ, and is forever in Christ, through his relationship with the Father. It has nothing to do with a price paid to buy something back. Rather, Christ himself has become deliverance. To be sure, Scripture speaks of a great price.[77] But the death of Christ was not a price that was paid. Death in itself is not a substance that can be offered.[78] Christ "became the source of eternal salvation" (Heb 5:9), not by the sacrifice of his death, but by offering himself, by dying toward the Father (cf. Heb 9:14). It is the Father who has supplied the great price,[79] a very dear price, and doubly so: dear to his heart and dear because of its value. Paul and John join forces in affirming this: "God so loved the world that he gave his only Son" (Jn 3:16; also cf. Rom 8:32).

According to Mark 10:45: "The Son of Man came not to be served but to serve, and to give his life as a ransom for many." Would his death, therefore, have nevertheless been a price paid to God? Consider that Scripture often says that God redeemed his people from the slavery of Egypt. No one would ever imagine that God would have "paid off" someone for that. Nor does Jesus claim to pay a ransom to God. Using language in the biblical sense,[80] the above passage from Mark could be translated like this: "Having come to serve, I give my life for the liberation of many."

Luke recalled the first part of this phrase ("come to serve"), but was not aware of the second part ("give his life as a ransom") (cf. Lk 22:27). Whatever the reason for this omission,[81] Luke was not aware of a redemption acquired in virtue of a price paid. In Luke's gospel, Jesus carried out his mission by departure (cf. Lk 9:31), by being taken up (cf. Lk 9:51), and by an entrance into his glory (cf. Lk 24:26). Everything was realized in Jesus himself.

Saint John did not say that the Son of Man must "pay for the world," but that the Son of Man must "be lifted up" (Jn 3:14). Jesus is *in person* the salvation of whom God made a gift to the world that he loves so much (cf. Jn 3:16). He is the light whose coming dispelled the darkness (cf. Jn 9:5). He is "the resurrection" (Jn 11:25). He is the Lamb who takes away the sin of the world by baptizing the world into the holiness of the Spirit, not by loading himself with their sin (cf. Jn 1:29–33). The Holy Spirit descended on him, not on sin (cf. Jn 1:32). Christ's redemptive death was honored in the Johannine writings as well as in the whole apostolic preaching. Jesus was the heavenly paschal lamb who would be sacrificed. The entire Gospel of John was focused on the hour of the Passover of the Lamb. But the meaning of his death was neither a price paid nor a punishment endured for the guilty. Jesus, who was consecrated by the Father from all eternity (cf. Jn 10:36), reached the summit of consecration through death, "I consecrate myself for them, so that they also may be consecrated in truth" (Jn 17:19) [NAB]. The work was finished in the person of Jesus through his relationship with the Father (cf. Jn 19:30).

It is sufficient to consider two texts from the Epistle to the Hebrews: "In the days of his flesh, Jesus offered up prayers and supplications, with loud cries and tears, to the one who was able to save him from death, and he was heard because of his reverent submission. Although he was a Son, he learned obedience through what he suffered; and having been made perfect, he became the source of eternal salvation for all who obey him" (Heb 5:7–9). The drama of salvation was his.[82] He begged to be saved and he was heard and made perfect through suffering. We are then saved in him who has become our salvation.

The author wrote further: "Since we have confidence to enter the sanctuary by the blood of Jesus, by the new and living way that he opened for us through the curtain [that is, through his flesh]" (Heb 10:19–20). The Jewish high priest entered once a year into the sanctuary through the veil drawn aside, carrying a vessel with the blood of the sacrifice. Jesus entered once and for all the sanctuary of God by means of his torn flesh, by virtue of his own blood. He was a forerunner (cf. Heb 6:20) and the pioneer (cf. Heb 2:10). Now he invites his faithful to set out on this "new and living way" by becoming, in person, the way of salvation.

In none of these texts do we see Christ satisfying the justice of God, offering a price, or undergoing punishment for sin in place of human beings. He did not reconcile God with humans. Rather, "in Christ God was reconciling the world to himself" (2 Cor 5:19). Redemption was a gratuitous gift, a work that God achieved. He achieved it in Christ, who became the mystery of salvation. Just as through his life and death, Jesus was "established as Son of God in power" (Rom 1:4) [NAB], he likewise became redemption, the very event of salvation (cf. 1 Cor 1:30). Because of his solidarity with the world, the salvation that was personal to Jesus is intended for everyone.

THE HOLY ONE IN SOLIDARITY WITH SINNERS

"He has rescued us from the power of darkness and transferred us into the kingdom of his beloved Son, in whom we have redemption, the forgiveness of sins" (Col 1:13–14). God begot his Son into the world of sin and made him one in solidarity with sinners. Paul expressed that solidarity between the Innocent One and sinners in view of justifying them with the phrase, "he [God] made him to be sin who knew no sin, so that in him we might become the righteousness of God" (2 Cor 5:21). God sent Jesus, the Innocent One, who was free of all sins (cf. Jn 8:46), "in the likeness of sinful flesh" (Rom 8:3).[83] The Son, whose name is glorious, was greatly deprived of glory, even to the point of being obliged to ask for it from his Father (cf. Jn 17:1). He thus found himself like sinners of whom it is said: "All have sinned and fall short of the glory of God" (Rom 3:23). Jesus shared with them existence "according to the flesh." That existence included the creature in his or her weakness, closed in on oneself, "enslaved to the elemental spirits of the world" (Gal 4:3),[84] subject to the law of Moses, and doomed to death. By itself flesh is capable only of sinning. That is why it is called "sinful flesh."

As a human being among human beings, Jesus shared to an eminent degree the call of all to become freely and fully children of God, which is what we are by the will of our creator Father.

By his death and resurrection, Jesus passed from flesh to life as Son in the Spirit. That Spirit is holiness and divine justice. At first "revealed in flesh, vindicated in spirit" (1 Tim 3:16), "he died to sin, once for all; but the life he lives, he lives for God" (Rom 6:10). The process of justification was accomplished on behalf of humans: "He died for all...and was raised for them" (2 Cor 5:15). Through faith rooted in Christ, the justification that is proper to Christ also became the justification of humans. All of this is summed up in an extremely concise expression: "He [God] made him to be sin who knew no sin, so that in him we might become the righteousness of God" (2 Cor 5:21). That means that through communion with the Christ of glory, we become the "justice of God," since he "was raised for our justification" (cf. Rom 4:25).

The Epistle to the Galatians offers two texts parallel to 2 Corinthians 5:21. On earth Jesus was subject to the law of Moses. His mission was to free those who were bound to this law, so that from being slaves they might become, in him, children of God in the Holy Spirit (cf. Gal 4:1–7). Just as Jesus passed from "the likeness of sinful flesh" to existence according to the Spirit, he likewise passed from slavery under the law to filial freedom. United to him, we are now beneficiaries of "the redemption that is in Christ Jesus" (Rom 3:24).

Another text of the Epistle to the Galatians (3:10–16) presents the passage from slavery to filial freedom in a dramatic form. The Galatians believed that salvation was found in the Mosaic observances, or at least in perfection at the end of one's life, thus making the unique mediation of Christ useless. Viewed from this aspect, the Mosaic law can appear as an adversary of Christ. Jesus was in solidarity with people upon whom lay the curse of the law: "Cursed is everyone who does not observe and obey all the things written in the book of the law" (Gal 3:10). This curse fell on Christ himself: "Cursed is everyone who hangs on a tree" (Gal 3:13). The law led Jesus to his death, "We have a law, and according to that law he ought to die" (Jn 19:7). But Jesus, who died by the law, also died *to* the law and was raised in the liberty of the Holy Spirit. In turn, the believer dies "by the law to the law" in communion with Christ who lives in him or her (cf. Gal 2:19–20). From now on, in Christ even pagans benefit from the blessing of Abraham (whom the law prevented from reaching), and as a gift of the Holy Spirit (cf. Gal 3:14).

These two texts from the Epistle to the Galatians thus offer a commentary on 2 Corinthians 5:21. In his existence according to the flesh, Jesus was in solidarity with sinful humanity and with those subject to the Mosaic law. Dead to the flesh and raised in the holiness and liberty of the Spirit, he bears along with himself those who are united to him in faith.

Saint John did not speak of Jesus' solidarity with sinners. Dazzled by his holiness, John seemed to be unaware of "the likeness of sinful flesh." However, in John's gospel. Jesus must "depart from this world and go to the Father" (Jn 13:1), from his worldly existence removed from life in the bosom of the Father. Although with the Father always (cf. Jn 10:30), Jesus still must go to the Father (cf. Jn 14:28). Heavenly (cf. Jn 8:23), he must ascend on high (cf. Jn 6:62). Already consecrated (sancti-fied), he longed for a higher consecration (cf. Jn 10:36). Per-forming glorious works, he asked the Father to glorify him (cf. Jn 11:40). No shadow of sin hovered over the holy one of God (cf. Jn 8:46). However, he lived as in a foreign land. At the mo-ment of entering his passion he used an expression similar to the words of the prodigal son: "I shall get up and go to my father" (Lk 15:18). Jesus also said, "I am going to my Father" (Jn 14:28).

According to the Epistle to the Hebrews, Jesus, who was "with-out sin" (Heb 4:15), "had to become like his brothers and sisters...to make a sacrifice and atonement [85] for the sins of the people" (Heb 2:17). Redemption was accomplished through his passage from abasement to glory via death: "But we do see Jesus, who for a little while was made lower than the angels, now crowned with glory and honor because of the suffering of death. So that by the grace of God he might taste death for everyone. It was fitting that God...in bringing many children to glory, should make the pioneer of their salvation perfect through sufferings. For the one who sanctifies and those who are sanctified all have one Father" (Heb 2:9–11).

All these texts confirm that salvation was effected in the per-son of Jesus through his death and glorification. Since he is for-ever glorified in his death, he is forever effecting salvation. But these texts say more. They say that this Christ-redemption is integrated into the human community. An authentic solidarity prevails between him—"the Holy One of God" (Jn 6:69), "who knew no sin" (2 Cor 5:21)—and sinful humans. He is not in solidarity with sin; otherwise he would be party to it. However, he is in solidarity with sinful humans. Like them, he must pass from flesh to spirit. For humans, this process is one of conver-sion. For Christ, it was one of transformation through death.

But solidarity with the sinful world was even deeper than suspected because no one realized the depth of the relationship between Jesus and other humans in their earthly condition. Every human is in solidarity with others by sharing the earthly condition. But only of Christ is it said: "We are convinced that one has died for all, therefore all have died. And he died for all, so that those who live might live no longer for themselves, but for him who died and was raised for them" (2 Cor 5:14–15). The only earthly condition of Jesus that was not included in solidarity was that which was very personal to him and naturally not shareable. However, all humans can share in his death and resurrection.

According to Johannine and Pauline faith, God creates humans in the role of Father of Christ. In other words, God creates us in the wake of the salvific Incarnation: "All things have been created through him and for him [Christ]" (Col 1:16). Creation belongs to Christ as its origin and its goal. Christ himself belongs to it, being "the firstborn of all creation" in whom "all things hold together."[86] That which belongs to Christ is destined for all humanity which was created "through him and for him" (cf. Col 1:15–17). For creation, Christ is the Son in his loving obedient death and resurrection. Thus, all can die and rise in his filial death and resurrection. Humanity, created by the Father in his Son, is sinful. In his very being, Jesus is in solidarity with humanity. He carried it in himself. He is in solidarity with it, not on account of sin, but by his divine begetting. He is in solidarity by the paternal act that begot him into the world and created the world amid the mystery of that begetting. Jesus is in solidarity because of being divinely begotten and, therefore, he is also in solidarity through holiness. He was in solidarity not only during his passion, but he is forever in solidarity with all other humans because of his submissive relationship to God.[87]

In the heart of the sinful world Christ is the leaven of sanctification, the opposite of sin. He turns sin around, and inverts what is an aversion to God. His mission is to make sinful humanity submissive to God, expiating its sins, according to the biblical meaning of the term, by consecrating humanity to God.

In order to understand the tragedy of Jesus' mission, it is useless to think of God's wrath venting itself on Christ who had become incarnated sin. Instead, we should consider the overwhelming number of sins whose burden he bore, and the holiness of the unlimited power to which he opened himself. That is what was necessary to carry sinners beyond the enormity of their sin and transform them into children of God. God's wrath was exercised against sin, not against sinners. Jesus never ceased to say that God loves sinners. God's wrath was not poured out on "my beloved Son with whom I am well pleased" (Mt 3:17; 17:5)[88] when he accomplished his mission.

THE EXPIATION OF SIN

"Christ died for our sins in accordance with the scriptures" (1 Cor 15:3).[89] One could think that a theology where everything is carried out by the entrance of Jesus into full filial communion does not take into account an essential aspect of redemption, the expiation of sin.[90] But the theology of the paschal mystery does not separate Christ's death from his resurrection. Rather, it explains the meaning of his death by its relationship to the resurrection. And that is where the expiation of sins is understood in its biblical truth and in its efficacy.

In modern language "to expiate" means to undergo punishment proper to the fault committed. Thus it is thought to be repaired.[91] But according to biblical language it is the divinity who expiates the sins of humans by his holiness.

"In French, as in a number of modern languages, the notion of expiation tends to be confused with that of punishment. On the contrary, for the ancients to say "expiate" is essentially to say purify, or more exactly to make an object, place, or person acceptable from then on to the gods....Expiation wipes out sin by reuniting the person to God, by consecrating him or her to God."[92]

On the Day of Atonement *(kippur),* the high priest "expiates" the people of their sins and consecrates them by sprinkling the sacred blood of the sacrifice (cf. Lev 16). The person does not heal his or her sin because another has satisfied divine justice through suffering. Similarly, a person does not become immortal through someone else dying in his or her place. Sin does not exist in itself in a way that it can be wiped away or guilt no longer imputed it. Sin exists only in sinful humans who are dead to eternal life. Their sin is expiated when God converts them, giving them the capacity to live in his life-giving holiness.

At the beginning of the Gospel of John, Jesus is referred to as the Lamb of God, the heavenly and true paschal Lamb. As such, he takes away the sin of anyone who enters into communion with him. Because the Spirit of holiness rests on him, he baptizes humans in that holiness (cf. Jn 1:29–31). At the climactic point of the gospel, John again evoked the Lamb, "None of his bones shall be broken" (Jn 19:36). From the pierced side there flowed the blood of the Lamb and water, a symbol of the Spirit in which Jesus baptizes (cf. Jn 7:37–39). Sin was taken away and humanity was "expiated" in the holiness of the sacrificed Lamb.

The language of Paul is different, but similar in its profoundness. The apostle protested when a shadow of sin was cast over Christ (cf. Gal 2:17). When Scripture says "for our sake he [God] made him to be sin for us" (2 Cor 5:21) and "sending his own Son in the likeness of sinful flesh" (Rom 8:3), it envisions the abolition of sin, not submission to punishment (about which Paul does not speak). According to John, Jesus took away sin by his holiness. Likewise, according to Paul, he abolished sin through the work that was the opposite of the sin of the first Adam (cf. Rom 5:18–19). "In him we might become the righteousness of

God" (2 Cor 5:21),[93] sharing the holiness that bursts forth in the Christ of glory.

According to the Epistle to the Hebrews, Jesus accomplished purification for sins (cf. Heb 1:3). He purified them by his blood, since "without the shedding of blood there is no forgiveness of sins" (Heb 9:22). That blood was not a price paid nor a punishment undergone for sinners. Rather, Christ was himself consecrated to God by the blood that he shed. "He entered once for all into the Holy Place...with his own blood, thus obtaining eternal redemption" (Heb 9:12).[94] The faithful are purified of their "dead works" by the sprinkling of the most holy blood of Christ.

To sum up, Jesus became *in person* the expiation of all sins. Sanctified by his immolation, he is now the sanctification of the world: "For their sakes I sanctify myself, so that they also may be sanctified in truth" (Jn 17:19). The expression "in his flesh he has made both groups into one and has broken down the dividing wall" (Eph 2:14) applies both to separation from God and separation among humans themselves. The blood he shed, that is, his own sacrifice, is the blood of the covenant by which sinful people were expiated according to the biblical meaning of the term (cf. Mt 26:28).

His blood was the instrument for the forgiveness of sins (cf. Mt 26:28). On numerous occasions when Scripture refers to "redemption, the forgiveness of sins," there is never evoked a price paid or a punishment undergone by Jesus to obtain this forgiveness (cf. Col 1:14). Jesus himself is, in his sacrifice, the forgiveness of sins, the crucible of the purification of sinners. That is why Jesus commanded us to "take, eat (Mt 26:26)," "this is my body which is given for you" (Lk 22:19), and "drink from it [this cup]...for this is the blood...poured out for many for the forgiveness of sins" (Mt 26:28). In effect he was saying, "Enter into communion with me," for in the holiness of the blood of

Christ, whose sprinkling they receive, and in the holiness of the immolated Christ, with whom they enter into communion, humans are "expiated." Their sins are forgiven in communion with Christ in his sanctification.

What was the meaning of the sufferings of Christ? In this context they are not a response to the demand of offended justice nor are they a punishment undertaken in the place of sinners. If that were the case, the pardon would not be gratuitous, and justice, carried out as humans tend to understand it, would take precedence over the fatherhood of God in regard to his Son. Love would be neither the first nor the absolute cause. However, the gift of holiness, in which the sinner is pardoned, asks to be accepted by the recipient. God made "the pioneer of their salvation perfect through sufferings" (Heb 2:10). He learned to consent to God: "He learned obedience through what he suffered and having been made perfect, he became the source of eternal salvation" (Heb 5:8–9). By themselves, neither suffering nor death glorify God. Yet, through them, God wishes to glorify Christ and all humans.

THE REDEMPTION AS PRAYER

The last word of Jesus on the cross as quoted by Mark is the beginning of Psalm 22: "My God, my God, why have you forsaken me?" (15:34). According to Luke, Jesus died taking up a prayer from Psalm 31 which he introduced by the word "Father," as is frequent in Luke's gospel, "Father, into your hands I commend my spirit" (23:46). One could think that these two gospels contradict each other: surrender to God in Luke, abandonment by God in Mark. According to the theory of substitution, the death of Jesus would have to be understood as a breach between God and Christ, who had been loaded down with the sins of the world. It would have meant an abandonment by God.

51

The prayer of Jesus, and the great cry he uttered when expiring, will never divulge their secret. However, theologians do not have the right to interpret a gospel text by contradicting the meaning the evangelist gave it. The idea of God abandoning Jesus did not cross Mark's mind (nor Matthew's who followed him). The passion account was interwoven with Scripture quotations, explicit and implicit, that are intended to refer to Jesus as the Messiah chosen by God, but rejected by humans. Psalm 22 was cited several times for this purpose.[95] It dealt with a just man who was persecuted by humans, yet miraculously helped by God. No one has ever thought that the psalmist was abandoned by God. His complaint was vehement, yet full of confidence, and concluded with a joyous thanksgiving. Would that quote on the lips of Jesus have a meaning contrary to the psalm from which it came? Only centuries later would this text—intended to present Jesus as the Chosen One of God—be interpreted as abandonment, or rejection on the part of God.

Mark's work begins this way: "The beginning of the gospel of Jesus Christ the Son of God" (Mk 1:1). It culminates in the great cry of Jesus as he dies, and the profession of faith of the centurion: "When the centurion, who stood facing him, saw that in this way he breathed his last, he said, 'Truly this man was God's Son!'" (Mk 15:39). The final prayer and the great cry provided the ultimate proof of the opening statement: "Jesus Christ the Son of God."

The distress of Jesus on the cross, like in Gethsemane, had to be immense, so much more crushing than that of the psalmist. But like the psalmist, Jesus addressed himself to "his God" and his God in turn to him. It was God who heard Jesus' cry of distress and changed it into thanksgiving. One may rightly conclude that the two prayers transmitted by Mark (Matthew) and Luke do not contradict each other. The Epistle to the Hebrews calls to mind the "prayers and supplications with loud cries and tears." God did not respond there with silence or censure. The epistle declares, "He was heard because of his reverent submission" (Heb 5:7).[96]

Is it possible to enter more deeply into this distress? Jesus invited his disciples to follow him. In their communion with him many of them experienced a similar distress. They uttered the same cry to God. But they had not been abandoned. When they left their "dark night," they felt themselves locked in the arms of their God and Father. Jesus, who always relied on his Father, did not fall into a void at the moment of his death. A child could moan, "Mother, why are you paying no attention to me?" But she is not really neglecting the child—after all, she is the one who gave it birth. Similarly, between the Father and the Son there is a radical distinction. It was necessary that one be the infinite Father and the other the infinite Son. That distinction is not a breach, but is absolute otherness amid infinite communion. Jesus, who was always the Son, took on infinite receptivity before the Father who shared his divine fullness. Christ's suffering and death shows how painful reception of the infinite can be.

According to appearances, the death of Jesus was not different from any sinner cursed by the law (cf. Gal 3:13), and doomed to death by his or her sin (cf. Gen 2:17). Theologians must not think like the high priests who stopped at appearances. There is a parallel between the paths of Jesus and the sinner, but in opposing directions. One is conversion toward God, of filial receptivity. The other is turning away, refusing the love and fatherhood of God. But the magnitude of these two directions is unequal. The filial receptivity of Jesus is infinite, going way beyond the negativity of sin, and is capable of reversing and absorbing sinful humanity into its holiness. The Johannine vision is grandiose: the immolated Lamb takes away the sin of the world.

Jesus died at the ninth hour (three o'clock in the afternoon). Those who handed on such precise information were Jewish Christians. They knew the importance of the ninth hour as the official hour of Israel's prayer. Jesus accomplished his work at that hour by praying.

Instead of resorting to the analogy of human justice that is so different from God's, why doesn't the theology of redemption let itself be guided by the analogy of prayer?[98] The Epistle to the Hebrews placed the redemptive drama within the framework of a prayer being heard (cf. Heb 5:7–9). It compared Christ's redemptive moment to the liturgy of entering the Holy of Holies on the Day of Atonement. Hence, the mystery of salvation is a liturgy in which all sins are forgiven.

The redemptive act and prayer are very much alike. They are both an ascent to God. Jesus ascended there on behalf of all, becoming prayer for us, an eternal supplication for our salvation.[99] Prayer is an entrance into communion. Through death, Jesus rejoined his Father, fulfilling in himself the covenant between God and his people. Prayer is an act of submission in which humans open themselves up to the fatherhood of God and let themselves become children to him. Jesus died begotten on behalf of all. He became redemption by becoming prayer.

Prayer results in grace, not because it offers gifts to God to which God has to respond with other gifts, but because prayer openly welcomes God's gift. The grace of salvation is likewise gratuitous, and Jesus opened himself up to salvation both for himself and for the world. The prayer of a Christian obtains salvation for others because it opens itself to grace and thus becomes for others a source of that grace. Jesus said: "For their sakes I sanctify myself, so that they also may be sanctified" (Jn 17:19). The mystery of salvation is that a person (Jesus) became prayer for the whole world, and it was heard.

Bypassing Juridical Theologies and Their Derivatives

Each type of theology is only an approach to God's mystery. Juridical type theologies do not offer an analogy with prayer. They are only a distant approach, and it is appropriate to by-pass them.

In juridical theologies the notion of justice is central, but it is understood in the way we humans exercise justice in our disputes. But we must remember that God's justice is transcendent. It is so different than ours, that it appears contrary to human justice.[100] God's justice comes from the holiness of God, who is revealed as love without boundaries, especially in the New Testament. Justice that is love has as its criteria neither "merit" that must be compensated nor "fault" that must be punished. It is gratuitous (cf. Rom 3:24). Such justice is exercised by communicating itself to the one who receives it: God wishes "to prove at the present time that he himself is righteous and that he justifies the one who has faith in Jesus" (Rom 3:26). For us to receive that justice, which was first attained by Christ, we must openly receive the gift of God. Theologies centered on badly understood divine justice are defective in their insistence on the need for restitution. It was God who paid the great price of redemption, not us. It was God who accomplished the expiation of our sins by sanctifying us human beings in his Son.

In juridical theologies the attention is focused on the forgiveness of sins obtained through the passion of Christ. Yet the messianic times were announced as a restoration of Israel with a profusion of the gift of the Holy Spirit. According to Paul, God inaugurated in Jesus Christ a new creation: "Everything old has passed away; see, everything has become new!" (2 Cor 5:17). In this newness, sin is abolished. Theories centered only on Christ's death do not take into account his victory over sin.

Yet, indeed, "if Christ has not been raised, …you are still in your sins" (1 Cor 15:17). A person dead to God cannot come to life again merely because someone else has died in his or her place.

If the essential reality of our salvation boiled down to the death of Jesus, Christianity would have its face turned to the past. But the real impetus of our faith focuses on a coming salvation: "You turned to God…to wait for his Son from heaven, whom he raised from the dead—Jesus, who rescues…" (1 Thess 1:9–10). Everything Christian is oriented toward eschatology.

If the death of Jesus had settled everything and destroyed sin, then why would we need a commitment to the work of faith (cf. 1 Thess 1:3) in the mystery of Christ's death and resurrection (cf. Rom 6:1–10)? If the death of Jesus had settled everything and destroyed sin, then it should be enough to believe that Christ paid the price and then rely on the justice of God which was satisfied by this price. Yet such a theology of justification contradicts not only the Epistle of James but the whole scriptural message.

Likewise we could ask, why would we need the sacraments? The proclamation of Jesus' death and the judgment pronounced on the cross against sin should be the only thing necessary. Less attention to the sacraments, as in certain churches that call themselves "churches of the Word," follows this logic of the juridical theories.

In the logic of these churches, the unique mediation of Christ is understood as exclusive, not allowing the faithful any participation in the redemption of the world (cf. 1 Tim 2:5).[101] Only Christ could pay the infinite price. Since it is paid, why a need to add more? However, the mediation of Christ, while we know that it is entirely unique, it is not exclusive. It is rich and inclusive. Christ has made the Church his body and enables it to share in the paschal mystery. The allegory of the vine and the branches is an illustration of this. Saint Paul was aware of being in communion with Christ in his death and resurrection for the life of the Church (cf. 2 Cor 4:10–12).

Let us consider one final criticism of juridical theologies, and indeed this is the most serious. Those theologies do not honor the Trinitarian aspect of redemption.[102] In them, God is not a father. Rather, he is identified with a justice that demands its rights. He is not a Father who begets. Instead, his justice demands the sacrifice of the Son. He does not act as a Father who first loves since it was necessary for humans to be reconciled to him, and that is the exact opposite of "in Christ, God was reconciling the world to himself" (2 Cor 5:19). The initiative, which had to go back to God as Father, is instead taken by Christ. In the theory of substitution, God turned against his Son at the moment when Jesus accomplished the mission he received from his Father.

Jesus is considered as Man/God but not Man/Son of God. Before Jesus, there is not a Father whose love he can accept, but a God who demands justice. He is not the Son who is received, but the Man/God who offers an infinite price, treating the Father as an equal. The Son pays, the Father then gives in return. In the theory of substitution, Jesus is not so much God's Son by his holiness, but is rather the universal guilty person. It is remarkable that while most religious persons think of themselves as sinners before God, Jesus never manifested such a feeling of culpability. He was never aware of any blemish. He was the beloved Son (cf. Jn 3:35) who was always in his Father's house (cf. Jn 8:35).

The Holy Spirit is ordinarily absent, in those theologies—obviously, since the Spirit is communion—a notion foreign to juridical thinking. The Spirit's absence in the theology of redemption has perhaps been the cause of the eclipse of the Spirit in western theology. The Spirit is the holy justice of love. Any theory where justice is not gratuitous love, bypasses the Holy

Spirit. But in neglecting the Spirit of truth (cf. Jn 14:17) who teaches everything (cf. 1 Jn 2:27), we remain far from the truth.[103] The theory of substitution speaks of a death-breach. In that way it denies the presence of the Spirit in the dying of Jesus, the Holy Spirit being communion. Given this fact, it ignores the sonship of Jesus in his death. It ignores Jesus as the Son of God in the Holy Spirit, as well. If so, Jesus died as a mere sinner, and what is the salvific value in that?

The substitution theory presents a strange image. Jesus is like one taken as a hostage. Is that not a barbarous act? In this theory, the God of truth considers Christ guilty, the very contempt of truth. Here, the righteous Father seems to practice a form of justice that contradicts the divine justice that Scripture says is exercised by communicating itself (cf. Jn 17:25). In fact, it contradicts all justice, since it strikes the innocent. Is not such a God turned upside down?

No text, unless badly translated or badly understood, guarantees these theories. The principal text referred to, 2 Corinthians 5:21, does not have the meaning some give to it.[104] Galatians 3:13 is clear in that the curse affecting Christ was not that of God, but of the law viewed in a hostile way toward faith. Every exegete knows that John 1:29 must be translated: "Here is the Lamb of God who takes away the sin of the world," and not "who carries sin." He takes sin away by his holiness as the heavenly paschal Lamb within whom the Spirit resides. He did not perform the function of a scapegoat who carries our sins.[105] The First Book of Peter (2:24), "He himself bore our sins in his body on the cross," is to be interpreted according to its imagery. An innocent person cannot carry the sins of others. Sin and the sinner do not exist apart from each other. A person can carry only the sins of which he or she is guilty. It is the burden of sinful humans that Jesus carried, those humans with whom he is in communion through the sanctifying holiness of his divine begetting.[106]

The meaning of his death showed itself from the beginning of Jesus' ministry. He is the Lamb of God who takes away sin by his holiness (cf. Jn 1:29). He let himself be baptized "to fulfill all righteousness" (Mt 3:15), the righteousness that he accomplished in his death. He proclaimed the Good News of the kingdom (cf. Mk 1:15) where "people will be forgiven for their sins and whatever blasphemies they utter" (Mk 3:28). At the end of his ministry, Jesus became *in person* the Good News of the kingdom where "we have redemption, the forgiveness of sins" (cf. Col 1:14). In all of this, there is question neither of a price paid to satisfy offended justice nor of a substitutive death. Just as "death has been swallowed up in victory" (1 Cor 15:54), so also was sin swallowed up in the holiness that erupted on this world in Christ.

The sanctifying holiness of God is always first. Considerations about sins to be expiated are second. God's holiness is a love without boundaries, and is totally gratuitous. It floods the world before any reparation of sin takes place. Sin is repaired, abolished by receiving God's love. And Jesus is the one who mediates receiving that love.

Theories in which the reparation of sin is the basis of thought are like believing that the Sun revolves around the Earth. Rather, it is love that is primary and that moves everything, including heaven and earth.

Chapter Five

EASTER AND THE SECOND COMING

I f everything had been settled by the cross, we would no longer have need of Christ, either now or in the future. Once the "merits" had been acquired, it would have been enough to delegate the Church to apply them to believers. Similarly, the second coming would be of minimal importance as a simple closure of history with Christ judging the salvation of some and the rejection of others. Then the door would close. The second coming would not comprise part of the mystery of salvation anymore than the Resurrection. But for the first Christian communities, the second coming was *the* awaited day of salvation: "You turned…to serve a living and true God, and to wait for his Son from heaven, whom he raised from the dead–Jesus, who rescues us from the wrath that is coming" (1 Thess 1:9-10).[107]

To be saved, a person must encounter the one who is salvation. The merits of Christ cannot be distributed. "To merit" is to dispose oneself for the gift of God, to open oneself to God. By dying, Jesus opened himself infinitely to God—that is not something that can be distributed or given out. What Christ merited was to be born to filial fullness. Salvation is realized in

Jesus—it is personal to him. Christ is effectively the savior of the world to the extent that he comes and gives himself to the world. The second coming is "the day of redemption."[108] It will be the time when a filial relationship will be granted to all (cf. Rom 8:23). Hope is bound up for us in the second coming: "Remembering…your work of faith and labor of love and steadfastness of hope in our Lord Jesus Christ" (1 Thess 1:3). Grace acts on the faithful by drawing them to the coming Christ: "You were called into the fellowship of his Son, Jesus Christ our Lord [in his day]" (1 Cor 1:9). Several members of the community at Thessalonica had died. The others thought they were lost since they died before the final coming. Paul reassured them that the second coming will be for them, too (cf. 1 Thess 4:13–18). Otherwise, they would be lost.

THE DAY OF THE LORD

"Lord" is Jesus' title both in his resurrection and his second coming. The last day, as well as every Sunday commemorating the Resurrection of Jesus, is called "the Lord's Day."[109] There is only one name for both events of the same mystery.

The power of the Resurrection has placed Jesus at the end of history. It manifested his salvation in its universal and final fullness. Everything else finds fulfillment in him. His resurrection was a resurrection from the dead (cf. Rom 1:4).[110] The last judgment was pronounced: "Now is the judgment of this world" (Jn 12:31).[111] The eschatological scene, when every knee will bend and every tongue will confess the lordship of Jesus, follows upon Jesus' obedience even unto death (cf. Phil 2:8–11). In his paschal glory, Jesus is the Lord of the Day.

The resurrection of the only Son was not only an anticipation and a prophecy—it is the eschatological mystery itself since "in him the whole fullness of deity dwells bodily" (Col 2:9).

Through the risen Jesus, final salvation is already in the midst of the world.

The faithful are also aware that "the night is advanced"; that they must conduct themselves properly as in the day (cf. Rom 13:12–13). In the middle of the night, the day is already appearing: "You yourselves know very well that the day of the Lord will come like a thief in the night....But you, beloved, are not in darkness, for that day to surprise you like a thief; for you are all children of light, and children of the day" (1 Thess 5:2–5). In the community, the presence of Christ is an object of both experience and hope, "which is Christ in you, the hope of glory" (Col 1:27). On the one hand, "you are of the day" since "your life is in Christ" (cf. 1 Cor 1:30). On the other hand, "the day is near" since its presence is veiled to a Church that is still earthly (cf. Rom 13:12). But the light passes through the veil—its presence is near and is coming.

THE LORD WHO IS COMING

Scripture uses two images to express the notion of Jesus' glorification: the image of exaltation and the image of the Resurrection. When these two images are put together, they allow for better understanding of his coming presence.

Jesus was lifted up from the earth (cf. Jn 12:32), glorified in God (cf. Jn 17:5), highly exalted (cf. Phil 2:9), far above...every name that is named (cf. Eph 1:21). He is no longer in the world (cf. Jn 17:11). In all these he is elsewhere, apparently absent. But without contradicting the image of exaltation, the image of resurrection removes the idea of absence. By raising him, God restored him to the world; he who had left it by death, but who is now unique by his death *to* the world. Jesus was both taken away and presented; elsewhere, yet coming from that elsewhere. This twofold movement is simultaneous, and its two parts provide for each other: Jesus comes to us by being elsewhere and, because he is elsewhere, where he has become a "life-giving spirit" (1 Cor 15:45), he is a being who gives himself. His coming to us is a result of his death which glorified him. Death, resurrection, and the second coming make up one unique mystery. In his death and resurrection, Jesus is both the event of salvation and its coming. He is salvation every time his death and resurrection is actualized and spread throughout the world.

Jesus announced the reign of God. He insinuated that the reign would come in his person (cf. Lk 11:20). But it was only through great suffering that the Son of Man would rise again (cf. Mk 8:31). The messianic coming was announced even more clearly than the resurrection from the dead, though the disciples did not understand (cf. Jn 20:9). His coming would take place "after three days," that is, without delay: "For as lightning flashes and lights up the sky from one side to the other, so will the Son of Man be in his day. But first he must endure much suffering" (Lk 17:24–25). Forming into one and the same image the exaltation to heaven and his coming (which equals the coming of the kingdom), Jesus declared, "From now on you will see the Son of Man seated at the right hand of Power and coming on the clouds of heaven (Mt 26:64).

In none of Jesus' sayings do the resurrection and the second coming appear as separate events.

Jesus departed by dying and returned through resurrection. He disappeared by dying and he appeared raised in a form such as he had never yet been seen. He did not merely appear after his resurrection, but he prolonged the whole process of rising.[112] His appearances were not a secondary or transitory phenomenon.[113] He was glorified not only in God, but in the world. By raising him, "God allowed him to appear" (Acts 10:40). Having been raised, Jesus came and appeared. Jesus had known an existence "according to the flesh" (Rom 1:3) which is an existence closed in on itself. Although he was even at that time under the aegis of the Spirit, the possibilities of his presence and his self-giving were limited. He had been sent only to "the lost sheep of the house of Israel" (Mt 10:6). He lived with his disciples at their side. Now he is sent to all nations (cf. Mt 28:19) and lives in the hearts of his disciples: "On that day you will know that I am in my Father and you in me, and I in you" (Jn 14:20). He now exists for the unlimited benefit of all, through the total gift of himself.

Such is the work in him from the Father by the power of the Spirit. The Father sent Jesus by raising him. He sent him in his paternity: Jesus is "the one whom the Father has sanctified and sent into the world" (Jn 10:36). The Father sent him by raising him in the world, by begetting him there. Jesus' consecration from now on is total and his mission is universal in the fullness of his begetting. Everything was accomplished in the Holy Spirit, who was the begetting power by whom the Father raised Jesus (cf. Rom 8:11). Jesus was flooded by the Holy Spirit.

It is noteworthy that from the earliest Christian times the disciples understood that Jesus died "for us." The formula never meant that he died in our place. If he died in place of humanity, what would be its advantage? If a person offers to die in place of a friend, the friend does not become immortal from it. Rather, the formula means "on our behalf." One might want to believe that his death was the price paid for our redemption. But Paul wrote: "For him who died and was raised for them" (2 Cor 5:15). His resurrection was certainly not a price that was paid. And so his death can no longer be understood in that way. In his death and resurrection Jesus is for us. He "pro-exists" for all, through the salvation realized in his person. In his saving death and resurrection, he comes to us and he gives us himself.

Eucharist, the eminent sacrament of the paschal mystery, reveals the meaning of the words *for us*: "This is my body that is for you" (1 Cor 11:24); take then and eat, for what I am in my Passover I am for you. Because his coming is still veiled, the Eucharist stirs up desire. The faithful say: "*Marana tha!* Come, Lord!" (cf. 1 Cor 16:22).

But Jesus did not come by returning. He rose without denying the mystery of the death by which he left the world. His coming does not nullify his leaving—it is not a return.[114] The Eucharist is the sacrament of the real presence of someone who is elsewhere, who is not of this world, except by the bread and wine that lend him visibility.

Jesus comes to the encounter by drawing us to himself. He gave birth to the Church by creatively summoning it to himself; by "eschatologizing it." That is how Jesus was first drawn toward his glorious paschal birth by the power of the Holy Spirit. It is by the same power that the bread and wine are still drawn toward Christ to become the sacrament of the eschatological meal.

Sometimes the Church is depicted as a period of time inserted between the mystery of redemption and the future *parousia*. In other words, the Church trudges along on earth from the redemption situated in the past where it derived its origin, until the return of Christ. But the paschal mystery is the event where the Church has its origin and will also find its perfection, as well. In his Passover, Christ is both Alpha and Omega for the Church at the same time. The point of departure and the end constitute one whole. In the same movement, without being divided into two opposite meanings, the Church goes toward its fulfillment: the second coming, and toward its source: Jesus, who is "the resurrection of the dead" in his death and resurrection (cf. Acts 4:2). The Church trudges on from the first encounter in communion to the communion of all; from its initial resurrection in Christ to the resurrection of all in Christ.

The second coming is the impact that the paschal mystery has on the world. It is the effective reality of Christ's death and resurrection for us. The Passover of Jesus founded the Church and leads it to its end. Sunday is "the Lord's Day." It is the Lord's Day in his resurrection and the Lord's Day in his final coming. It was considered both the first and the eighth day of the Christian week. It is the day of the Eucharist, which is the sacrament of Jesus' Passover and of his coming presence.

As the day of Passover and the second coming, it is also the day of the outpouring of the Holy Spirit.

HE BAPTIZES IN THE HOLY SPIRIT

By raising him, God sent Christ. God raised him in the superabundance of the Holy Spirit and sent him to pour out that Spirit: "When God raised up his servant, he sent him first to you to bless you" (Acts 3:26). That blessing was the gift of the Holy Spirit (cf. Gal 3:14) who had not been bestowed before that moment: "As yet there was no Spirit, because Jesus was not yet glorified" (Jn 7:39).[115]

The prophets announced the outpouring of the Holy Spirit like a beneficial rain, or a gushing spring.[116] Christ is both the Father's promise,[117] and the Spirit's promise (cf. Acts 1:4, 2:33).[118] Jesus died to rise again (cf. Jn 10:17) and to enter into the glory (cf. Lk 24:46) that is the Holy Spirit[119] and to communicate that Spirit: "Being exalted, therefore, at the right hand of God, and having received from the Father the promise of the Holy Spirit, he has poured this out" (Acts 2:33). Jesus died in order to give us the Holy Spirit.

According to the gospel of the Lamb of God, upon whom resides the Holy Spirit (cf. Jn 1:29–33), Jesus promised that he would make the Spirit spring up in the heart of his faithful one like the water of eternal life (cf. Jn 4:14). Later, he invited the faithful one to drink the water that will spring from his own side. The feast of Tabernacles commemorated the spring that flowed from the rock and that will also spring up at the time of the Messiah. "On the last day of the festival, the great day, Jesus was standing there, he cried out, 'Let anyone who is thirsty come to me, and let anyone who believes in me drink. As the Scripture has said: "Out of the believer's heart shall flow rivers of living water."' Now he said this about the Spirit which believers in him were to receive; for as yet there was no Spirit, because Jesus was not yet glorified" (Jn 7:37–39). The rock was there. It was only necessary that it be struck for the waters to spring up from it. Jesus renewed the promise and announced its accomplishment.[120] The last breath of the Crucified One symbolized the divine breath that he poured out while raised above the earth (cf. Jn 19:30). The water that flowed from his side along with the blood confirmed the promise of the feast of Tabernacles.

While he was on earth, Jesus did not give the Spirit: "It is to your advantage that I go away, for if I do not go away, the Advocate will not come to you; but if I go, I will send him to you" (Jn 16:7). The Spirit was the one on high, the quintessence of divine holiness. Its origin was in the heavenly Father. The gift of salvation was given in the humanity of the Son where salvation was realized. Jesus had to be glorified in his humanity by the Father and become heavenly even in his body. Then rivers of living water will flow from within him (cf. Jn 7:39). Moses struck the rock and the waters flowed. The lance of the soldier opened the side of Jesus raised above the earth and the rivers of the Spirit poured out on the world. Humans "will look on the one whom they have pierced" (Jn 19:37), they will look up to the last day and will be invited to drink from the spring of the open side (cf. Rev 1:7).

The Spirit is not offered as a gift outside of the giver. In fact, this gift is inseparable from the donor. Jesus gives the Holy

Spirit—from whom he lives, and in whom he is the Son. He gives it by coming to us, and by giving himself. Jesus showed his wounds and his side from which he said that the rivers of the Spirit would spring up (cf. Jn 7:37–39). Water is a symbol of the Spirit, and it had flowed. The Breath of God, announced by the last breath of the Crucified (cf. Jn 19:30), poured out on the disciples: "He breathed on them and said to them, 'Receive the Holy Spirit'" (Jn 20:22). His coming in their midst as foretold, brought the Spirit who had been promised (cf. Jn 14:17–18). The Spirit of communion (cf. 2 Cor 13:13) is given in communion with Christ—in his coming—which is inseparable from the Son whom the Father begets Jesus and sends him through the Holy Spirit.

As Son, Jesus has received the Holy Spirit from the Father, who is the source of that Spirit, and offers it to us. We humans receive the Spirit through our own union with Christ, forming one and the same body with him in death where the Father has filled him with the Holy Spirit. This gathering of humans, reunited in Christ and the Spirit, is called *Church.*

Chapter Six

THE BIRTH OF
THE CHURCH

T o speak of the Church after discussing Christ in his Passover and his coming is not really a new topic. Jesus rose,
and with him a great crowd. The paschal mystery that
involves the second coming is also ecclesial. Having been raised,
Jesus comes into the world in his body that is the Church.

THE CHURCH,
THE BODY OF CHRIST IN HIS COMING

From the start of his time on earth, Jesus was open to others.
He had the potential to become a community of salvation. The
reign of God that opened up a path from the days of John the
Baptist (cf. Mt 11:12) worked in him with power (cf. Lk 11:20).
Jesus gathered twelve young men about him—a symbol of the
new Israel, the twelve tribes. The messianic marriage was inaugurated (cf. Mk 2:19), the mustard seed was sown, the kingdom
of God was among them (cf. Lk 17:21).

The reign, however, was yet to come: "There are some standing here who will not taste death until they see that the kingdom of God has come with power" (Mk 9:1). That reign was

present in the person of Jesus, and in his person it will come again in power. The coming of the messianic community had been proclaimed as being similar to the son of man "coming with the clouds" (Dan 7:13). Jesus personalized that symbol, claimed the title Son of Man, and announced at the start of his passion: "From now on you will see the Son of Man seated at the right hand of Power and coming on the clouds of heaven" (Mt 26:64).[121]

Shortly before his death, after the Jewish crowd had acclaimed him, some pagans expressed the desire to meet Jesus. His joy exploded: "The hour has come for the Son of Man to be glorified" (Jn 12:23). That glory would consist in bearing much fruit.[122] Like the grain of wheat, Jesus would die and rise—both as himself and as a great crowd (cf. Jn 12:24).

Jesus enjoined the high priests: "Destroy this temple and in three days I will raise it up" (Jn 2:19). They would destroy the temple built by human hands (cf. Mk 14:58). By being torn in two, the veil of the temple announced that destruction (cf. Mk 15:38). Jesus would rebuild it without delay "in three days." Having been raised, he would be God's dwelling among his people, the gathering place, the place of encounter with God, and the place of sacrifice and praise. His temple would not be earthly. There worship would be conducted in spirit and truth (cf. Jn 4:23).

The kingdom "comes in power" in the person of the "Lord of glory," and is identical to him. One can, therefore, speak of the kingdom of the Son (cf. Col 1:13), where the Son himself is the kingdom. The second coming of Christ is still expected in the world. Yet the earthly Church already forms part of his kingdom. The Church is the kingdom's initial and growing presence, preparing its members to become fully the kingdom of God.

Saint Paul says the Church is the body of Christ. He also compares human society to the human body where every member plays its role for the good of the whole. Paul uses that comparison (cf. 1 Cor 12:12–26), and goes so far as to make the Church the very body of the risen Christ: "As the body is one and has many members, and all the members of the body, though many, are one body, so it is with Christ" (1 Cor 12:12).

"Now you are Christ's body, and individually members of it" (1 Cor 12:27). The many are taken into and unified with Christ by the power through which he rose. That power is the Spirit: "In the one Spirit we who are all baptized into one body" (1 Cor 12:13). We are gathered into one body that existed even before we were gathered. We were baptized[123] into Christ, we clothed ourselves with Christ and have become one in him (cf. Gal 3:27–28). Christ is the Lord of the "church, which is his body" (cf. Eph 1:22–23).

Paul is the only one to define the Church as the body of Christ. Perhaps he had that intuition thanks to his experience of the Eucharist: "The cup of blessing that we bless, is it not a sharing in the blood of Christ? The bread that we break, is it not a sharing in the body of Christ? Because there is one bread, we who are many, are one body" (1 Cor 10:16–17), the body of Christ.

The Church was founded *in* the Resurrection of Jesus, not after it. The temple was not rebuilt after the Resurrection—the grain of wheat that died was reborn in abundance. In begetting the Son into glory, God begot him by multiplying him—the multitude who were raised along with him (cf. Col 2:12). God gave a body to his Son who died for all—his own body that is also the Church. Thus the Church is always linked to Christ's beginnings because Christ lives forever from the moment of his full birth in eternity.

The mystery of the Church can be understood by another image that complements the body. By raising his Son in death, God gave him a spouse who would form one body with him:

"The Lord...gave his blood for the one whom he would obtain in the resurrection."[124] "The one whom he would obtain" is, according to Augustine, the bodily humanity of Christ as well as the Church. Ephesians 5:32–33 calls to mind Genesis 2:24: "A man...and his wife...become one flesh" and comments: "This is a great mystery, and I am applying it to Christ and the church" (Eph 5:32). Earthly marriages model a marriage where "the savior of the body" takes to himself the Church. They are the shadow projected on earth of the heavenly union between Christ and the Church. In making the faithful his body, Jesus did not take away their personality. Two spouses do not stop being two persons when they "become one flesh" (Eph 5:31). "It is Christ who lives in me," says Saint Paul. But he adds: "I live by faith in the Son of God" (Gal 2:20). He is also one person. The Church is not passive—it permits Christ to be what he is—spouse and head. In the power of the Holy Spirit, who raised Jesus and gave him to the Church, the Church receives him as her spouse. However, she who receives everything is willing to receive Christ—and she lets herself be married.

IN DEATH AND RESURRECTION

The marriage was celebrated at the hour when Christ became the savior of the body, as he "gave himself up" for the Church and became salvation in person (cf. Eph 5:23–25). At that moment the Church was introduced into the communion of his death and resurrection.

The two formulas "in Christ" and "with Christ" used by Paul are complementary. The first determines the existential framework of the faithful: "You *are* in Christ" (1 Cor 1:30) [NAB]. We exist in him. The second describes how Christ and the Church live together, namely, in the union of death and resurrection, or in realizing our salvation.

Baptism introduces a person into communion with Christ—
"baptized into one body" (1 Cor 12:13)—and is a participation
in his death and resurrection: "Do you not know that all of us
who have been baptized into Christ Jesus were baptized into
his death?...so that, just as Christ was raised from the dead by
the glory of the Father, so we too might walk in newness of life"
(Rom 6:3–4). Through baptism we are buried in him, and die
with him the same death, and we are also raised with him.[125]

Eucharist confirms the faithful in their union with the immolated and glorious Christ. Saint Paul transmitted the words
of institution of the Eucharist in this way: "This cup is the new
diathēkē in my blood" (1 Cor 11:25). By the word *diatheke* (or-
dinance, institution, or arrangement) the Greek Bible translates
the Hebrew *berît* (covenant), meaning that the covenant with
Israel was not a simple pact between two partners. Rather, God
instituted that relationship with authority, marked by the blood
of Christ. The Church was established by God in Jesus' Passover. The covenant was sealed in the sacrifice of Jesus who includes within himself the Church.

Jesus was raised without leaving the mystery of his death.
The Church permanently lives a communion of death with him:
"I have been crucified with Christ" (Gal 2:19) in sufferings (cf.
Rom 8:17), in trials, in apostolic labors (cf. 2 Cor 4:10–12). At
the end of life on earth, death will consecrate all who are in
union with Christ into a full communion of death with him: "If
we have died with him, we will also live with him" (2 Tim 2:11).

The Church also knows "Christ in the power of his resurrection and the sharing of his sufferings by becoming like him in
his death" (Phil 3:10). The eschatological mystery of the resurrection is at work in us.[126] God does not incessantly repeat the
action of resurrection on our behalf—that action was unique,
and it is exercised in begetting the Only Son. We are raised by
"the power of his resurrection," the same power that gives life

to Christ in his death. Christian existence is eschatological, rooted in the coming fullness of salvation.

To the definition "the Church is the body of Christ," we must add the following clarification: It is by sharing in his death that the body of Christ enters into glory.[127] In that way one rediscovers the Johannine vision whereby Jesus draws all people to himself from above his glorious cross (cf. Jn 12:32–33). There the Church is like a flock led by a shepherd who gives his life for the sheep. In the Book of Revelation, the shepherd is an immolated lamb.[128]

AN ASSEMBLY CALLED TOGETHER IN THE SPIRIT

The gathering of people brought together is called *ekklēsia,* that is, an assembly called together, or brought together, by summons. The members are "saints called to be holy."[129] Christianity is a calling. This word is used with an extraordinary frequency, sometimes redundantly: "The calling to which you have been called" (Eph 4:1)

It is to a person that we are called. We "are called to belong to Jesus Christ" (Rom 1:6) and "called into the fellowship of his Son, Jesus Christ our Lord" in his day (1 Cor 1:9). This call is formative—it "calls into existence things that do not exist" (Rom 4:17). It creates communion with the Son, calling each of us to be apostles and saints (cf. Rom 1:1,7). It produces justification (cf. Rom 8:30), leads one to freedom (cf. Gal 5:13), and peace as one body (cf. Col 3:15)—the body of Christ: "In one Spirit we were all baptized into one body" (1 Cor 12:13).

In his paschal mystery, which includes the second coming, Christ comes to the encounter. He comes by calling and he calls by drawing. He draws from atop his glorious cross (cf. Jn 12:32–33); he calls and draws by making himself seen. That is how the Church was founded. That is how the Church will reach its fullness: "When he is revealed, we will be like him, for we will see him as he is" (1 Jn 3:2).

The call to communion is another name for grace. The Pauline principle that we are saved by grace and not by works becomes, in Romans 9:12, "not by works but by his call." God is constantly "the one who calls us,"[130] who draws and gathers together in his Son those whom he begets for the world.

A call, and a force of attraction are images describing the Spirit. The formula "in the Spirit" is frequent in Pauline literature, as well as that other formula "in Christ." The two have a reciprocal relationship: "Anyone who does not have the Spirit of Christ does not belong to him" (Rom 8:9). God calls people to Christ, incorporates them, and gives them life in Christ by the Holy Spirit through whom he raised Jesus. The power of Christ's resurrection is the grace by which the faithful live.[131]

John was a theologian who recounted the mystery and described it in symbols. He increased the use of those symbols at the place where his gospel reached its highpoint: in the account of Jesus' death. On Calvary, the messianic nation was present in the person of Mary, just as she was previously at the first miracle of Cana. After Jesus had completed the plan determined by the prophecies, he declared: "It is finished," and to say that he expired, the evangelist used the strange phrase: "He gave up his spirit [the Spirit]" (Jn 19:30). Raised on the cross above the earth, symbolically exalted to heaven, Jesus gave up the Spirit. He did not let his head sink to die, rather "He bowed his head." Toward whom? Toward his mother and the disciple standing near the cross. On them he poured out the Spirit. What was described by these symbolic gestures was actually carried out on Easter evening: "He breathed on them and said to them: 'Receive the Holy Spirit'" (Jn 20:22).[132] That is the Johannine account of the birth of the Church.

The Church is unceasingly born of the Spirit in the filial

mystery of death and resurrection. The Father begets us not by repeating his paternal action on our behalf. He has only one Son into whom all other humans are assumed. God raises us in our own company. God does not adopt us—he begets us because in Christ the resurrection was not an adoption. God is creator Father, not adoptive Father: "We are what he has made us, created in Christ Jesus" (Eph 2:10), "born anew"…through the Resurrection of Jesus Christ…"not of perishable but of imperishable seed" (1 Pt 1:23). Saint John insists: "We should be called children of God; and that is what we are" (1 Jn 3:1).To be born of God in the Holy Spirit is a more genuine birth than to be "born not of blood or of the will of the flesh" (Jn 1:13). The Holy Spirit, in whom we are born, enables us to become aware of the reality of our relation to God: "But when the fullness of time had come, God sent his Son…so that we might receive adoption (filiation). And because you are children, God sent the Spirit of his Son into our hearts, crying, 'Abba, Father!'" (Gal 4:4–6).[133]

The Church was thus constituted in the unity of Christ raised in the Holy Spirit:"All of you are one in Christ Jesus" (Gal 3:28); "to gather into one the dispersed children of God" (Jn 11:52). We were dispersed in space and time. The Spirit brings us back from all corners of the earth and has us all live in one same instant the death of Christ in which we are born with him. In its mystery the Church is born today in this place and this time. It will also be born tomorrow. It lives at the source and, as long as it is on earth, it lives from it more and more.

It seems necessary to offer clarification on the difference between the Only Son and those of us who share in Christ's loving obedient relationship to God. In his humanity, Jesus was assumed into the Word, who is the eternal Son. The faithful are not immediately assumed into the eternal Son, but into the humanity of Jesus where the mystery of their salvation is realized. Paul is speaking of Jesus in his human "I" when he says: "Christ who lives in me" (Gal 2:20). Jesus is the subject of the Christian life. In Christ, there exists a human "I" that forms part of his human nature.[134] That is the center of his being where he is self-aware and from where he makes decisions. Jesus humanly lived his relationship to his God-Father from that center, and opened himself up in his death to the power of resurrection. It was there that he was given the charge to gather together the many and make them into his body, sharing with them his death and resurrection. The Church is not Christ—it is only his human body. But it is the body in which he lives his death and resurrection.

FROM THE FIRST TO THE LAST TESTAMENT

Well before the death of Jesus there was a Church, a gathering called by God for his praise (cf. Ex 12:16),[135] to which the Acts of the Apostles alludes when it speaks of "the congregation in the wilderness" (Acts 7:38). The disciples of Jesus discovered the presence of Christ in it and recognized a Christian character about it. According to the Gospel of Luke, Jesus had "interpreted to them the things about himself in all the scriptures" and "opened their minds to understand the scriptures" (Lk 24:27, 45). The Risen One, who showed himself in the Cenacle, also made himself seen in the pages of Scripture. They stated that the book that nourished their faith, as well as the institutions and the history of which it speaks, were occupied with the presence of the One in whom they recognized their Lord.

God had begun to leave himself when he created the world. Then he began to speak to Israel. To speak is to leave one's self through the word that is begotten. God was preparing to set up a tent for his Word. He had recorded these multiple words and these enacted laws in their sacred books, making incarnate there, so to speak, the divine wisdom (cf. Sir 24:23). God went to far as to pronounce his name and in this way handed himself over to Israel, for God's name is God himself in his revealed mystery.

God transformed the people he assembled into his first-born son (cf. Ex 4:22); for "out of Egypt I called my son" (Hos 11:1). Israel carried hidden in its bosom the Christ who was to be born. "Now the promises were made to Abraham and to his offspring; it does not say, 'and to offsprings,' as of many; but it says, 'and to your offspring,' that is, to one person, who is Christ" (Gal 3:16). Paul reasons this way while knowing full well that the descendants of Abraham are a multitude (cf. Gen 17:4–8). But he sees the multitude contained in Christ, holder of the promises made to this multitude. Israel possessed Christ, while the pagans "were at that time without Christ, being aliens from the commonwealth of Israel, and strangers to the covenants of promise" (Eph 2:12).

God promised David that he would be a father for his descendant, Solomon, and the whole dynasty: "I will be a father to him, and he shall be a son to me" (2 Sam 7:14). But according to Hebrews 1:5 that proclamation was announced only to he who truly is the Son. The same holds true for: "You are my son; today I have begotten you" (Ps 2:7).[136] In the psalm, however, the phrase is addressed to a king of the Davidic dynasty. That meant that the dynasty was messianic, and that it was so because of the One who was to come. All the promises were carried out in the Resurrection of Jesus: "What God promised our ancestors he has fulfilled for us, their children, by raising Jesus, as also it is written in the second psalm, 'You are my son; today I have begotten you'" (Acts 13:33).

Israel was a maternal nation, the mother of Christ according to the flesh. She was a church composed of those who carried in themselves the messianic bud. Chapter twelve of the Book of Revelation presents the Church under the symbol of a woman crowned with twelve stars. Twelve, along with its multiples, is the ecclesial number. This Woman-Church, clothed with the sun, has her place in heaven: "A great portent appeared in heaven" (Rev 12:1). She was clothed in mystery and is pregnant. She was such from the start of history. Before her stands the serpent from the Book of Genesis (cf. Rev 12:9). She carries in her womb the messianic seed of Genesis 3:15 as interpreted by Christian tradition. She gives birth in her flesh and in faith to the promise. Paul says of Isaac, a child conceived in flesh and in faith, that he was "the child who was born according to the spirit" (Gal 4:29). That is what Jesus would also be in fullness.

"But when the fullness of time had come, God sent his Son, born of a woman" (Gal 4:4). In Mary, who is the mother of Jesus according to the flesh and by the Spirit (cf. Lk 1:35), the Church of the first covenant found its perfect symbol. The promises made to humanity through Eve focused on a group of people that became more and more limited. First it was a race, the Semites, to whom God's interest was directed (cf. Gen 9:20). Then it was a people from this race, those of Abraham, Isaac, and Jacob. Then it was a tribe of the people of Jacob, that is, Judah (cf. Gen 49:10). Then it was a clan of this tribe: David (cf. 2 Sam 7:14). At the very summit of this pyramid, there was a young girl engaged to a man of this clan. The invitation to messianic joy often addressed to "the Daughter of Zion," that is, the Jewish nation, was brought to this young girl: "Greetings, favored one!" (Lk 1:28). God's favor for Israel was centered on her in whom the maternal vocation of the whole nation was summed up. The Church of the first covenant was linked to Christ according to the flesh and by faith in the word of God. Saint Augustine said, "Jesus is the substance of this people, for he draws from them the nature of his flesh."[137]

Reading Scripture and the history of Israel, Paul distinguished the surface realities which he called "the letter" and the profound mystery, or "the spirit" that a follower discovers in looking at Christ, for the Lord is that Spirit (cf. 2 Cor 3:17). According to Saint Paul, the first institutions were the shadow of Christ who was to come: "These are only a shadow of what is to come; but the substance belongs to Christ" (Col 2:17).

The transition from the old to the new covenant was carried out in Christ himself. There existed a symbolic holy place in the heart of the temple in Jerusalem (cf. Jn 11:48). Because it was the symbol, its fate was linked to that of the Messiah: "Destroy this temple and in three days I will raise it up" (Jn 2:19). The high priests would destroy that temple which was the focus of attention in the dispute and from which Jesus had driven the sellers. In three days—that is, without delay—Jesus would re-build it. The evangelist explained: "But he was speaking of the temple of his body" (Jn 2:21). That temple built by humans would give way to a temple not made by hands (cf. Mk 14:58). The risen Jesus would be the holy place where people will "wor-ship in Spirit and truth" (Jn 4:24).

When Jesus died, "the curtain of the temple was torn in two, from top to bottom" (Mt 27:51), announcing that it was empty of the Presence that had inhabited it. With the substance of the people being gone, the house collapsed. The first temple found its fulfillment in his raised body which was the passage and the link between the covenants.

The Lucan account of the birth of Jesus evokes only the Daughter of Zion; the fourth gospel is more explicit. Mary was not called by her personal name there, but by a functional name —she personified a community and its history. She was Jesus' mother (cf. Jn 2:1). Jesus called her by an unusual word: "woman."[138] She had come on the scene when at Cana the hour of Jesus, who was the passage from the first covenant to the new one, was announced: "There was a wedding in Cana of Galilee, and the mother of Jesus was there" (Jn 2:1). She reappeared when the hour to depart struck (cf. Jn 13:1). "Standing near the cross of Jesus were his mother..." (Jn 19:25). She was the faithful companion of the Messiah in his Passover despite the defection of the Jewish leaders. Judaism's maternity, in both flesh and Spirit, was found centered in this woman. Her motherhood then crossed over entirely into the realm of the Spirit when Jesus proclaimed, "Woman, here is your son" (Jn 19:26).

In communion with Jesus who is "the substance of this people," the Church moved in Mary from the first covenant to the new covenant. The first was not abolished—it was fulfilled (cf. Mt 5:17). The water in the six jars at Cana was not emptied—it was transformed into wine. "*This* temple" that the high priests would destroy—*it* was what Jesus would rebuild. The same woman represented the first and the new covenant. The first Church, linked to Christ in the flesh, is forever with God in the mother of Jesus, who is its symbol.

The unity of the two covenants was sealed in the unity of the body of Christ, which is the substance of both. The difference is inscribed in him: first in his earthly existence, then in his heavenly and universal existence. The passage from one to the other was made eternal in Christ, in his death and resurrection.

Since then Jesus has called all people to enter into his Passover: "And I, when I am lifted up from the earth, will draw all people to myself" (Jn 12:32). He began through Israel. He drew it to himself in his mother, who is the maternal symbol of the nation. She was the first companion at his Passover. She also witnessed to the unity of the first and the new testament.

Jesus proceeded toward the encounter with people of former times whose future he had been and called them to himself. Matthew 27:52–53 shows "the saints" of former times following Christ in his passage from death to resurrection.[139] Catechesis in the first centuries recognized Jesus' descent into hell.[140] Christ "put to death in the flesh, but made alive in the spirit...went and made a proclamation to the spirits in prison" (1 Pet 3:18).[141] "...the gospel was proclaimed even to the dead" (1 Pet 4:6).[142] The Epistle to the Hebrews praised the faith of the ancestors to the promises of God. But "all of these died in faith without having received the promises, but from a distance they saw and greeted them....Yet all these...did not receive what was promised, since God had provided something better so that they would not, apart from us, be made perfect" (Heb 11:13, 39–40). The just one of former times and those of the new covenant enter the fatherland together. They enter by communion with the Passover of Jesus.[143]

Because the two covenants are united in the body of Christ, our faith can see them both in a single glance. God speaks to his Son in both, and speaks about him. The prophets of Israel viewed God's reign from what they knew of Israel's institutions. For example, the model of David's kingship was merely prolonged into an eternal kingship.[144] The messianic temple was seen to be like the Jerusalem temple (cf. Ezek 40–48). Zerubbabel, who rebuilt the temple after the exile, gathered the praises of the Messiah ahead of time.[145] Certain titles of the Risen One (for example, Messiah, Lord, Son of God) were sometimes attributed to kings.[146] This entire people of Israel already were children of God (cf. Hos 11:1).

The disciples of Jesus reversed the perspective, reading Scripture from the vantage point of the Risen One. They attributed to Jesus, and to him alone, texts concerning Israel—its institutions, its kings, and its just ones—giving those tests a fullness of meaning without precedent. To Christ alone fell the honor of filiation (cf. Heb 1:5) that had been previously given to Israel[147] and the Davidic dynasty. To the Son alone fell the title of God (cf. Heb 1:8) that Psalm 45 attributed to a king.

From atop the glorious cross Jesus drew to himself the first covenant, its people, its sacred Scriptures, its temple, and all the people who had died before him. He did not abolish anything. Rather, he carried everything along, transforming it all, just as he himself had passed from the flesh to the Spirit. He reduced the law of Moses, that contained 613 commands and prohibitions, to its essential and basic demand: love of God and neighbor. A new moral order was established.

Chapter Seven

JESUS' PASSOVER AMONG THE FAITHFUL

S aint Paul described his existence in Christ this way: "I have been crucified with Christ; and it is no longer I who live, but it is Christ who lives in me. And the life I now live in the flesh I live by faith in the Son of God, who loved me and gave himself for me" (Gal 2:19–20). The Christian is a believer. He or she puts faith in the Son of God who handed himself over for us.

A LIFE OF FAITH

Such faith was awakened in the first disciples by the Resurrection of Jesus. Exegetes and theologians ask how "paschal faith" was born,[148] and offer a variety of causes: the scripture according to which Jesus said he must rise (cf. Jn 20:9); a rereading of the life and sayings of Jesus; his appearances; or the empty tomb. The first cause is the Risen One himself in his encounter with his own friends. That encounter was both interior—"you will know that I am in my Father, and you in me, and I in you" (Jn 14:20)—and it was made concrete by his appearances. The disciples had an encounter and they knew it. They believed because they saw him. The Risen One, toward whom faith is made, also brings about that faith. Thus, Mary Magdalene, Thomas, the disciples at Emmaus, and Paul became believers "when God…was pleased to reveal his Son to (them)" (Gal 1:15–16). It is still that way today. A person becomes and remains a believer through an encounter. And no proof is entirely convincing apart from any encounter: "No sign will be given to it except the sign of the prophet Jonah" (Mt 12:39).

Faith is born in communion and lived in communion. The transcendent One makes himself known by becoming present. The disciples took on Christ after having already been taken on by him (cf. Phil 3:12). They saw Christ as he made himself visible. They believed because of the One who gave them life (cf. Gal 2:20) and who was their life-giving spirit. Faith in the Risen One results from the power of the Resurrection through which Jesus was able "to make all things subject to himself" (Phil 3:21) and was able to submit everything to obedience in faith (cf. Rom 1:5). The power that raised Jesus produces faith in him—the one who has been raised. The Spirit glorifies Jesus in itself and in the world: "No one can say, 'Jesus is Lord,' except by the Holy Spirit" (1 Cor 12:3). The faith of Christians results from the glorification of Jesus, and the radiance of his glory in the world.

It is toward the Risen One that faith is made, faith that the power of resurrection arouses. Faith does not automatically proceed toward certain truths.[149] It does admit the truths it knows to be revealed. But mainly, faith clings to the Risen One who teaches those truths. The apostles were not primarily propagators of religious truth. Rather, they were the heralds of someone. Their preaching was a *kerygma*, a proclamation: "We proclaim Jesus Christ as Lord" (2 Cor 4:5). Jesus is the Word in person to whom a believer submits. If the apostles' discourse was in any way dogmatic, it was that this Word is light for us (cf. Jn 1:4). The faithful say: "We have come to believe in Christ Jesus" (Gal 2:16).

The Christ who is preached is Christ the savior, the one who is "for us," the mystery of salvation in death and resurrection. Faith proceeds toward him not only because the fullness of divinity resides in him, but because that fullness is also meant for human beings.[150] "It will be reckoned to us who believe in him who raised Jesus our Lord from the dead, who was handed over to death for our trespasses and was raised for our justification" (Rom 4:24–25).

Jesus is the resurrection of the dead *in person*. That's what makes him the object of faith: "I am the resurrection and the life. Those who believe in me, even though they die, will live....Do you believe this?" (Jn 11:25–26). Faith flows toward the person of Christ to whom the faithful follower clings, and to the truth articulated by him. The truth he articulates is secondary, but it is based on Jesus who is the resurrection. It is to Jesus, lifted up above the earth like the serpent in the desert, that the glance of any believer is directed (cf. Jn 3:14). "They will look on the one whom they have pierced" (Jn 19:37), the one who "will draw all people to myself" (Jn 12:32).

Faith is an act of communion with Christ in his paschal mystery. The disciple believes in Christ as in the frequent formula where the Greek preposition *eis* shows movement toward Christ. Through faith, the disciple comes to Christ, drinks at the spring gushing forth from his pierced side, and slakes one's thirst from the abundant waters of the Spirit (cf. Jn 7:37–39). When Jesus presents himself as bread from heaven, the faithful are invited to eat that bread (cf. Jn 6:27–29). Faith welcomes and receives it. "His own people did not accept him. But to all who received him, who believed in his name, he gave power to become children of God" (Jn 1:11–12).

The believer enters by identifying with Christ—by participating in his death and resurrection. Therefore, every act of faith is a paschal communion. In the language of the synoptics "to believe" is to follow Christ even to death: "If any want to become my followers, let them deny themselves and take up their cross" (Mt 16:24). "The bread that I will give for the life of the world is my flesh" (Jn 6:51). That means one cannot live on the sacrificed body without being assumed into the sacrifice. Through faith, as Saint Paul lived in Christ, he was also crucified at the same time (cf. Gal 2:19).

Death "to the flesh" results from the power of the resurrection. By bringing us to life, the Risen One enables us also to die with him who was raised in death. We die to ourselves by the same power through which Jesus died and was raised, that is, by the Holy Spirit. "In him (the Christ of glory)...you were buried with him in baptism, you were also raised with him through faith in the power of God, who raised him from the dead" (Col 2:11–12).

In this communion we are justified. Jesus, who was first "revealed in flesh and vindicated in spirit" (1 Tim 3:16), was filled with God's redeeming justice for us. In communion of faith with Christ, the human person in turn becomes God's righteousness (cf. 2 Cor 5:21). Hence Paul no longer availed himself of the numerous merits gained by the observance of the Mosaic laws: "I regard them as rubbish, in order that I may gain Christ and be found in him, not having a righteousness of my own that comes from the law, but one that comes through faith in Christ, the righteousness from God, based on faith. I want to know Christ and the power of his resurrection and the sharing of his sufferings by becoming like him in his death" (Phil 3:8–10).

A person is not justified by his or her works. Justification is a gratuitous gift. However, one must collaborate with it and receive it through faith. By obedience even unto death, Jesus aided the inrush of the Father's sanctifying holiness into himself. All believers do the same in the process of their justification. They are open and receptive to God's holiness.

Faith is an obedient, receptive virtue. Believing is meritorious in the sense that to merit is to receive, or to embrace the gift, and let oneself be begotten. Justification is gratuitous, but it is granted only if it is embraced. That is true for the entire Christian life (cf. Phil 3:8–12).[151]

Faith is not only a mere belief—*it believes.* It is not a collection of truths articulated at the beginning of the Church that are still accepted today, although maybe not understood. The grace of faith is a revelation, an unveiling—it enables one to know. The paschal mystery is an epiphany: "...and again a little while, and you will see me" (Jn 16:17). Jesus made himself visible so that the disciples could offer him their faith. In the beginning Christ's appearances had an exceptional clarity which was necessary to found the Church. Today Christ reveals himself through the sacramentality of the Church, but it is always in revealing himself that he arouses faith. During his earthly life the eyes of the disciples had already penetrated the mystery: "to whom can we go? You have the words of eternal life. We have come to believe and know that you are the Holy One of God" (Jn 6:68–69).

We often speak of the "veil of faith," presuming that it prevents us from perceiving the whole mystery since at this time that mystery is still unveiled only incompletely in our earthly condition. Yet it enables us to see with the eyes of one's heart (cf. Eph 1:18). "And we have seen and do testify that the Father has sent his Son as the savior of the world" (1 Jn 4:14). That truth was not seen with bodily eyes, nevertheless it was truly seen. Saint Paul even has the boldness to say: "When one turns to the Lord, the veil is removed...all of us, with unveiled faces, seeing the glory of the Lord" (2 Cor 3:16–18).

IN LOVE AND HOPE

Faith knows the mystery because it has communion with it. In every act of faith, there is always at least a spark of love. Faith knows the mystery by intuition through the love that shares it: "To you has been given the secret of the kingdom of God, but for those outside, everything comes in parables" (Mk 4:11). Everything appears foreign to the stranger, everything is familiar to the family member.

The Holy Spirit of Jesus' Resurrection is the power of love. It is, therefore, the Spirit of truth who will guide us to the truth (cf. Jn 14:7; 16:13). The Spirit brings us into Christ (cf. 1 Cor 12:11) and enables us to know the truth.

Faith and love dwell in us with reciprocal influence. Faith devoid of love is demonic: "Even the demons believe—and shudder" (Jas 2:19). They know that Jesus is the Holy One of God, but they say: "What have you to do with us?" (Mk 1:24). Depart from us. On the contrary, the believer is the thirsty one who comes to Jesus (cf. Jn 7:37). The believer approaches out of love through the power of the Spirit of love: "No one can say, 'Jesus is Lord,' except by the Holy Spirit" (1 Cor 12:3).

That is why among the theological virtues love is held highest: Love believes everything (cf. 1 Cor 13:7). Saint Polycarp was able to write: "Faith is followed by hope and preceded by love."[152] Love is the summit as well as the cement of the foundation. That is a typical characteristic of Christianity: the end is also the beginning.[153]

Like love, hope is inseparable from faith. To believe in the one who is salvation *in person* is to place all one's hope in that person. Believers are "people of hope,"[154] persons who have "a new birth into a living hope through the resurrection of Jesus Christ" (1 Pet 1:3). Their God is the God of hope (cf. Rom 15:13) who gives us hope (cf. 2 Thess 2:16).

Hope is often named in third place.[155] Hope takes its point of departure in the loving faith by which one possesses Christ and the salvation that is in him: "Your life in Christ Jesus, who became for us...redemption" (1 Cor 1:30). But we possess Christ now only imperfectly. We are "called into the fellowship (communion) with his Son" (1 Cor 1:9), which will come to its fullness only in his day. In virtue of the initial gift, we aspire to fullness, certain of attaining it since the first installment has been given to us (cf. 2 Cor 1:22). We say, *Marana tha*, O Lord, come! (cf. 1 Cor 16:22) to the one who is already in our midst: "Christ in you, the hope of glory" (Col 1:27). Hope is loving faith that sets out toward the heavenly homeland in which it has already dropped anchor.

Hope consists of the desire for salvation with the certainty of obtaining it. That certainty came from the earnest promise of the Spirit: "Hope does not disappoint, because the love of God has been poured into our hearts through the Holy Spirit that has been given to us" (Rom 5:5). Hope dwells in our hearts along with certainty. The Spirit is hope as much as it is love, a love in search of the total communion. We "who have the first fruits of the Spirit, groan inwardly while we wait for adoption" in its fullness. God "knows what is the mind of the Spirit" (Rom 8:23–27), and will hear it. Love has hope in all things (cf. 1 Cor 13:7).[156]

Faith, hope, and love are "three and one" after the image of God the Father, Son, and Holy Spirit. The Father and the Son are one in the unity of their Holy Spirit. The trilogy is undivided in a love that is the soul of the other two.

Undivided, they are eternal. The charisms of the earthly Church, for example, prophecy and the gifts of tongues and of knowledge, will be done away with, like everything that is not personal communion with God (cf. 1 Cor 13:8–10). But "faith, hope, and love abide" (1 Cor 13:13). Faith and hope will not expire in eternity—they "abide." Could these two virtues that provide the basis on earth for life eternal be transitory? Faith is the door that receives salvation—it will never be closed. In his death Jesus lifted himself to the heights of an obedient faith at the summit of which he once again entered eternity. On earth faith was the first glimmer of eternal knowledge; in heaven it will attain all its brilliance.[157] Hope will reach the end for which it was aiming and will settle there, forever at the summit of an eternal desire that God has heard. "And the greatest of these is love" (1 Cor 13:13). Love animates the other two. It is not only produced in someone by the Spirit, it is also a mysterious participation in the Spirit: "God's love has been poured into our hearts through the Holy Spirit that has been given to us" (Rom 5:5).[158]

In heaven the eucharistic meal will be fully realized. That is where faith opens the hand, the mouth, and the heart to embrace the Passover of Jesus. Love rejoices at communion with his holy body, and hope sighs, *"Marana tha!"* There each person will live where hope and its fulfillment come together in an unsatiable overabundance.

CHRISTIAN ETHICS

The Holy Spirit who animates the three virtues governs the entire Christian life. "The Holy Spirit is in person the law of the New Testament."[159] The same law that rules the activity of God governs our activity. The Spirit is the one to whom Jesus submitted; Jesus who "was led by the Spirit" (Lk 4:1), who was offered to God in the Spirit (cf. Heb 9:14), and was raised by the Spirit (cf. Rom 8:11). Jesus let himself be led by the Spirit because he had been conceived in the Spirit. By submitting to the law of the Spirit, Jesus reached filial fullness. It is the same for us: "All who are led by the Spirit of God are children of God" (Rom 8:14). Christian ethics has a great noble character: the

Spirit's law is divine and it makes others divine. Humans are born children of God by submitting to the law of the Spirit.

Such a law is not written and cannot exist except in the heart: "I will put my law within them, and I will write it on their hearts" (Jer 31:33). Jesus said that the law of the Spirit springs up in the heart as a fountain of eternal life (cf. Jn 4:14).

As Christians, therefore, we must follow the law in our own heart. We are not to perform deeds because they are commanded by God. We must follow the law of our own being and do what we like, for our law is the spirit of "God's love that has been poured into our hearts through the Holy Spirit" (Rom 5:5). We are able to do what we like and what we must do because the law of love that governs us is the all-powerful Spirit of the Resurrection of Jesus.

"The law of the Spirit of life in Christ Jesus" (Rom 8:2) is, therefore, a law of liberty. Is there a person freer than the one who has the duty and the ability to do what he or she likes? "For you were called to freedom, brothers and sisters" (Gal 5:13). The salvation realized in Jesus is a redemption, that is, a liberation. By being raised in the Spirit, Jesus came into fully loving obedient freedom beyond all earthly restraints: "Where the Spirit of the Lord is, there is freedom" (2 Cor 3:17). In Christ, we are freed from the Mosaic law and every law external to our persons.[160] "For freedom Christ has set us free" (Gal 5:1). When we give consent to the Spirit, "love, joy, peace, patience, kindness, generosity, faithfulness, gentleness, and self-control" grow in us as naturally as fruit grows on a tree. "There is no law against such things" (Gal 5:22–23).

Free in Christ and in the Holy Spirit, we are subject to God. We live in the Spirit who is the will of God amid the love that is the commandment of God. One submits to God in proportion to one's freedom, because the love of the Spirit is equally submissive to God, and to others. The law of the Spirit allows us to freely give ourselves, just as Jesus did when he died and then was raised.

"The law of the Spirit of life" is also the reward that God grants to anyone who carries out this law. To be able to love is the joy of the one who loves—such a person asks for no higher reward. Jesus was heard in death, a death that was glorifying, and was rewarded in dying toward the Father. Death and resurrection constitute a single mystery.

All this finds its ultimate truth only in fellowship, or communion, with the Son (cf. 1 Cor 1:9). Christian morality is eschatological by nature, the law of the Spirit of life is a grace that calls us to that communion. The degree of freedom for any Christian is in proportion to the depth of his or her life in the Spirit. On earth, a Christian is still largely dependent on the flesh: "The life I now live in the flesh..." (Gal 2:20). To the extent that a Christian is not yet submissive to the law of freedom, that person is bound by multiple written laws contained in Scripture, such as the Decalogue, that are intended to regulate personal relationships with God and neighbor. That person is also subject to laws written by the Creator in human nature. Paul, while the herald of Christian freedom, still demanded submission to the civil power (cf. Rom 13:1–7), insofar as it conformed to God's authority. He also imposed on his communities rules of a canonical order (cf. 1 Cor 8–11; 14). These laws are "laid down not for the innocent person but for the lawless and disobedient..." (1 Tim 1:9), for those who do not yet live entirely by the Spirit. These laws are warnings and are not "the new and living way" (Heb 10:20) that comes from Christ raised from the dead. Those laws continue to play a role in our lives until Christ comes again,[161] that is, up until the day when Christ's law[162] triumphs, the law of the Spirit of the paschal mystery (cf. Gal 3:24, 6:2).

To sum up: the basis of Christian ethics is liberty from written laws external to the person. Yet, we are still subject to such laws. But the law of love and freedom must be primary. *The others are relative. They are at the service of love and freedom, subordinated to the good of the person in his or her relationship to God and neighbor.*[163]

THE COMMUNION OF SAINTS

To the extent that we live Christ, we are no longer "flesh," locked up within ourselves. Rather, we are spiritual (cf. 1 Cor 2:15). The Spirit, who is the law of the New Testament leads us to live in communion. By the creative power of the Spirit we are incorporated into Christ (cf. 1 Cor 12:13) who, dead to the flesh, is now our life-giving spirit (cf. 1 Cor 15:45). We live in mutual communion of existence and life: "All of you are one in Christ Jesus" (Gal 3:28).

Saint Paul knew that in the ecclesial community "we do not live to ourselves, and we do not die to ourselves" (Rom 14:7). Grace that is personal to each also belongs to others. "You hold me in your heart, for all of you share in God's grace with me…in my imprisonment" (Phil 1:7). Paul shares grace and in some way is its mediator: "In Christ I became your father through the gospel" (1 Cor 4:15); "My little children, for whom I am again in the pain of childbirth" (Gal 4:19). Paul is a father through his apostolic activities, but his paternity is based more on his communion with Christ than on his work: "We are always being given up to death for Jesus' sake, so that the life of Jesus may be made visible in our mortal flesh. So death is at work in us, but life in you" (2 Cor 4:11–12).

Sometimes the communion of the saints is represented as sharing the merits of following Christ who also shares his own merits. But merits do not exist by themselves and cannot be shared. The communion of saints is certainly a communion of persons in their mutual connectedness. Rather than shared goods or merits, Vatican Council II described the communion of saints as the bond of "His Spirit...[who] form one church and cleave together in him" (LG 49).[164]

The Spirit of communion is the "creator Spirit." The Spirit's presence creates communion. The Spirit is the love of the Father and the Son, and unites them within the indivisibility of its person. Poured out into Christ and the faithful, the Spirit unites them in the unique body of Christ and in its own unique person. The Spirit further personalizes Jesus in his humanity, making him universally relational.[165] He does likewise for us, each at our own level. Jesus rose—both as himself and as a great crowd. We do likewise according to the intensity of our communion with Christ.

We thus mutually enrich each other. There is no wealth as great as mutually belonging to each other. In the Trinity each person exists and lives through the others. Solitude can be deadly —communion is life-giving. The Spirit gives life by uniting us. Its grace is both maternal and fraternal.

According to the Gospel of John, there exists a woman who represents and sums up the Church. She is the preeminent Christian, the sister who is very close to all and is their mother. On the cross, Jesus uttered: "Here is your mother" (Jn 19:27). Sanctified fully for the Church, and thus sanctified for us all, she is the glowing heart of the maternal and fraternal community.

Human love gives us a glimpse of what happens when the Holy Spirit is poured out into Christ and the faithful. When two people love each other, one is enriched by the other and enjoys the gifts of the other as well as his or her own. If one is from a higher class, he or she raises the other to that class: a king makes the woman he marries a queen. Between two spouses who have loved each other over long years, a union is established that is not merely sentimental—it affects them in their being. The "I" of each is built upon their relationship and makes them inseparable. That is the desired effect of love. The Holy Spirit is a love who desires and is the powerful creator of what it desires. The Eucharist, the sacrament of the paschal mystery, is the preeminent sacrament of the communion of saints. In this sacrament we do not distribute or apply merits. Rather, Christ gives himself and enriches us. Giving himself, he joins us to himself and unites us mutually in his body (cf. 1 Cor 10:16–17) by the bond of the Holy Spirit. Christ makes us into what he is: beings who share themselves in mutual connectedness.

A basic equality, therefore, prevails among us in spite of our differing levels of grace. The holiness of the saints does not make them remote from the rest of us because their holiness belongs to us all. The holier they are, the more they share with others because of their holiness. We do not envy the saints—we thank them for being saints because they honor and bring happiness to us all.

The communion of saints extends its grace even beyond the borders of the Church. Saint Paul advised the spouse who became Christian not to separate from the spouse who remained pagan if the latter agrees to remain with him or her: "For the unbelieving husband is made holy through his wife, and the unbelieving wife is made holy through her husband" (1 Cor 7:14). The non-Christian world belongs to Christ and the Church through the love that connects Christ and the Church to the world. By raising Christ in the power of the Spirit, the Father not only made him head of the Church—he set him, together with the Church, into the heart of the world.

NOTE ON AN ECCLESIOLOGY OF COMMUNION

The Church in its perfection is subject only to the law of the Holy Spirit. On earth it is faithful to itself to the extent that it seeks to adapt itself to its heavenly truth. It must sail in the wake of its future in obedience to the basic law of communion with the Holy Spirit. For the anchor has already been dropped in heaven (cf. Heb 6:19), we have already been transferred "into the kingdom of his beloved Son."(Col 1:13).[166]

Through our communion in the Holy Spirit, the members of the Church are all equal. Jesus announced: "You have one teacher, and you are all students" (Mt 23:8). The differences that oppose or separate us in this world have been done away with: "There is no longer Jew or Greek, there is no longer slave or free, there is no longer male and female" (Gal 3:28). All share the same grace and dignity, the same power of the Holy Spirit. Therefore, in communion one does not find either superiors or inferiors—all are members of the body of Christ, animated by the Holy Spirit.

On earth the Church is also an organized society—it is an institution. The risen Jesus charged Peter to feed the flock (cf. Jn 21:15–17); he built his Church on Peter and the Twelve (cf. Mt 16:18). Paul advised: "Respect those…who have charge of you in the Lord" (1 Thess 5:12).[167] The Epistle to the Hebrews demands: "Obey your leaders and submit to them" (Heb 13:17).[168]

How can one bring together this Church that is a mystery of communion rooted in equality with an institution where superiors exercise authority? Two approaches to the Church are possible, depending on whether one gives priority to the institution or to the mystery of communion.

The Church was born out of the death of Jesus. Each person will understand the Church according to the meaning one gives to Christ's death. A juridical theology of redemption makes the institution and its power dominate over the principle of communion.[169] Having acquired a treasure of merits through his death, Christ has now delegated his powers to certain disciples who administer the Church in his absence. They manage what he acquired, they distribute his merits, they remit the debt of sins in virtue of that delegation. In that system, the Church has a two-class structure, one governing the other: the shepherds and the flock, the teachers and those taught, the ministers of the sacraments and the beneficiaries. In such a system one speaks a great deal about jurisdiction—the word communion is hardly or not at all mentioned.

But according to a theology of the paschal mystery, Christ's death was related completely to the resurrection and is inseparable from it. By dying, Jesus did not leave his own people. Rather, by his death and resurrection he came to them. He did not delegate powers, he communicates himself, claiming those who are his own as his own body that was sacrificed and given life by the Holy Spirit. The Church is the eschatological community that is joined together in the communion of the Holy Spirit. But it lives on earth where a society cannot exist unless it is structured and organized. Yet the institution is secondary and is at the service of communion. Authority exercised in this system draws its legitimacy from that service and is Christian only if it is inspired by communion.

Jesus did not write anything, since he was the book that God gives us to read. Jesus wrote the charter of the Church in the sacrament of himself that is the Eucharist. Eucharist presents the double aspect of institution and mystery, but with the obvious subordination of the institution to the mystery of communion. The faithful gather in a place determined by earthly space and time. They conform to established rites, and under the presidency of a member of the community, they take a meal of bread and wine, "fruit of the earth and the work of human hands." Without the institutional aspect there is neither Eucharist nor the Church of Christ on earth. But in the Eucharist the institutional aspect is secondary. It is merely a garment made to measure, to clothe and express the mystery so that communion with

Christ among the faithful may be realized from earth. Here the Church, the institution is also secondary to the mystery. The mystery of Christ seeks to express and realize itself through the earthly institution. "The Eucharist [that] makes the Church" should always be the primary starting point for any type of canonical legislation.

The Eucharist is celebrated by everyone, it is "the common property of the faithful."[170] The command "Do this in remembrance of me" (Lk 22:15, 1 Cor 11:24) was given to everyone through the apostles who symbolize the entire Church. "They offer the divine Victim to God, and offer themselves along with it. Thus, both by the act of oblation and through holy Communion, all perform their proper part in this liturgical service, not, indeed, all in the same way but each in that way which is appropriate to himself."[171] And so, the Scripture about having one teacher is proven (cf. Mt 23:8). Those who preside place themselves in the midst of the celebrating Church, not above it. They are in the midst, for their ministry is given by Christ to the whole Church, and exercised by the presider on behalf of the whole Church. Anyone who would try to preside at the Eucharist by deliberately putting himself apart from the rest of the Church would have no power to consecrate the bread and the wine.[172] In the presider, the Church receives from Christ the power to consecrate and distribute the Eucharist. In a particular way the Church acts *in persona Christi* in the presider as all the faithful celebrate the Eucharist *in persona Christi*.[173] The presider's role is essential. It would be futile to claim to have Eucharist without a priest, for the Church's ministry to celebrate the great culminating activity of Eucharist is conferred upon and centered in the ordained priest.

But their ministry does not raise them above the rest of the faithful nor does it place them in opposition to them. The priests's ministry is the ministry of the entire Church. If their ministry is distinct from the ministry of others, it is so only because it is central. But it is totally integrated.[174] The priests's ministry culminates profoundly in service of the communion of all into the mystery. In presiding at Eucharist, priests do not exercise power *over* the assembly. Their ministry is the fullness of the ministry that Christ conferred on the Church as a whole.[175]

Whoever would exercise power *over* the Church, a power of domination, would be in error about the nature of authority. He would commit a sin similar to someone who would use the Eucharist like an ordinary meal, without discerning the body of Christ (cf. 1 Cor 11:18–29). Ministry, as well as the life of the Christian, is marked by the sign of Jesus' death, similar to the lordship that Jesus announced in washing the feet of the disciples.[176]

Saint Paul knew "a still more excellent way" (1 Cor 12:31) with regard to all the charisms proper to the Church on earth. Love is the expression of the Holy Spirit's presence in the Church. True power is love that is mysteriously at work in the Church.[177] The power of love is common to all the faithful. It is proper to each one in his or her relationship with God and hence will not pass away (cf. 1 Cor 13:13). If different people seem to share differently in the power of love, they are different really only in the degree of love.

The Church is both sanctified and sanctifying. It has become the body of Christ from where the rivers of the Holy Spirit spring (cf. Jn 7:37-39).[178] In union with Christ, the Church is sanctified by receiving what it gives to others of the presence of the Holy Spirit. "Receive the Holy Spirit" (Jn 20:22), said Jesus, and by him forgive sins (cf. Jn 20:23). Would the Spirit be present and active in the universal sacrament of salvation (the Church and in particular the sacraments) if it were not received by the Church and its members? We can, therefore, think that anytime grace is dispensed by the Church, it is the whole Church who is benefiting from the grace. Grace dispensed by the Church sets up the ability also to receive that grace according to the degree of loving faith uniting one to Christ in his death and glory.

According to the Gospel of John, a woman was present near the cross with a disciple whom we presume was an apostle. For the evangelist that woman represents the Church. The Church and all its members are "the Jerusalem above...our mother" (Gal 4:26). She is the mother of all, even of the elevated members of the hierarchical institution.

In a Church that is both institution and mystery, primacy must always be given to the mystery, and that includes the Church as mother to us all, as well as the fraternal and maternal grace coming from the communion of saints. In the very depths of its being, the earthly Church is ruled by the same law as the heavenly Church. The authority proper to the institution is subject to the mystery from which it proceeds. Its authority is at the service of the mystery and must adapt as much as possible in exercising its power to the basic law of the Holy Spirit. Such authority will be Christian and sanctifying for those who exercise it.

We can expect in the future, that the theology of redemption will be free from juridical molds. We hope that an ecclesiology based on a theology of redemption will move on from ways of thinking and practice dominated by the delegation of powers and jurisdiction toward one where communion with Christ in the Holy Spirit prevails.[179]

The Church is unceasingly invited to that kind of conversion.[180]

Chapter Eight

AT THE SERVICE OF THE SECOND COMING

C hrist the Lord is coming in his death and resurrection because the paschal mystery is linked to the second coming. The Church is the Body of Christ in his death and resurrection. The Church is also sent: "As the Father has sent me, so I send you" (Jn 20:21). So the Church is at the service of Christ's second coming.

THE CHURCH SENT TO THE WORLD

Jesus called twelve young people to himself "to be with him and to be sent out" (Mk 3:14). In this way he began to found the Church—a Church that is with him and that is sent. He had numerous disciples, but Matthew, who is called the evangelist of the Church, spoke of the Twelve as being *the* disciples.[181] He saw in them a symbol of the Church. In the Cenacle, they did not represent only the future bishops and priests—they were "the living symbol of the new people of God."[182]

The Church will always remain intrigued by the number twelve. Consider the woman crowned with twelve stars, or the city that measures twelve thousand stades in length and width.

And Scripture counts twelve gates on which are written the names of the twelve tribes of Israel. In the Book of Revelation, there is a wall that "has twelve foundations, and on them are the twelve names of the twelve apostles of the Lamb" (Rev 21:14).[183]

In his paschal mystery, Jesus is the universal apostle (cf. Heb 3:1) sent by the power of his resurrection. Just like him, all disciples are sent. Mary Magdalene became a messenger through her encounter with the risen Lord. Jesus sent the Eleven after appearing to them gathered in the Cenacle and on the mountain in Galilee. After recognizing him "in the breaking of the bread" (Lk 24:35), the disciples at Emmaus went on to proclaim him. Paul was also sent after his vision: "Am I not an apostle? Have I not seen Jesus our Lord?" (1 Cor 9:1). God revealed his Son to Paul "so that I might proclaim him among the Gentiles" (Gal 1:16). United to Christ, Paul was led "in triumphal procession" (2 Cor 2:14) with him. Whoever encounters Christ in the power of the resurrection is also sent with him. The Christian vocation is of itself apostolic. Peter did not become first a disciple and then an apostle. His vocation as disciple was to become a fisher of people (cf. Mt 4:19). Through his conversion Paul was "called to be an apostle" (Rom 1:1)[184] just like all disciples "who are called to be saints" (Rom 1:7). For Paul, being an apostle was the way to be a Christian.

SHARING IN REDEMPTION

The Christian is, first of all, an apostle because he or she lives in communion with Christ. Jesus has not only paid the price of salvation, he has become salvation by bringing it about. He incorporated the disciples into himself and made them his own body in his salvific death, and in his "resurrection from the dead" (Romans 1:4). Christ gives them a share in the great salvation event. "And he appointed twelve…to be with him" (Mk 3:14). They were with him where he was in the redemptive mystery: "As he is, so are we" (1 Jn 4:17). The Church "is in Christ Jesus, who became for us…redemption" (1 Cor 1:30). With him and in him the Church is in the world which is the crucible of salvation.

The Eucharist is an illustration of the Church. The Church realizes and defines itself by that meal—a Church in participatory communion of the redemptive Passover: "This is my body which is given for you" (Lk 22:19), in order that you become what you receive. The disciples were brought into and included in that mystery whose sacrament is the Eucharist.

The understanding of Church in juridical type theologies is vastly different than this. In them, once having been acquired, redemption is up to the Church to proclaim and to manage the treasury of Christ's merits, "applying" them to the faithful through the sacraments.[185] The work of salvation is seen as unfolding in two distinct actions: (1) its acquisition and (2) its application to others through the ministry of the Church. The faithful benefit from redemption without participating in it, either for themselves or for others.

But the work of salvation does not unfold in two separate actions whereby Christ's second coming completes his first. Rather, it has been and is entirely accomplished in Christ once for all. In his Passover, he is the Alpha and the Omega of salvation. The event of salvation is also *his* event, and the paschal mystery is linked to the second coming. Jesus, who died for us and was raised for us (cf. 2 Cor 5:15), comes to us through his death and resurrection. And the Church is fully integrated into the mystery of salvation that is always on its way to fulfillment.

The Church adds nothing to the mystery of salvation, it does not complete it, and it is not a second act. The Church participates in everything through its role in the unique redemptive action of Christ. What Christ is, what he says and does, the

Church is also saying and doing in complete deference to Christ, in a communion that identifies the Church with Christ, who is the unique and universal mediator by his Passover. The apostolate of the Church is not a post-paschal activity, but is an aspect of the paschal mystery linked to the second coming as it spreads over the world. Through his death for all and resurrection for all, Jesus is both "sanctified and sent into the world" (Jn 10:36) in the Church that is his body.

Saint Paul was aware that we share in the mystery of salvation: "Always carrying in the body the death of Jesus…so that the life of Jesus may also be made visible in our mortal flesh. So death is at work in us, but life in you" (2 Cor 4:10–12). By being in Christ (cf. 1 Cor 1:30), the Christian shares in the mystery of redemption, for he or she constitutes one reality (cf. Gal 3:28) with Christ in his death and Resurrection.

Without communion the activity of the Church would be useless: "Apart from me you can do nothing" but "those who abide in me and I in them bear much fruit" (Jn 15:5). Christ, who is the vine, matures the fruit of salvation on the shoots.[186]

Along with the allegory of the vine, the Gospel of John gives a human symbol of the Church. The image of the Church as the mother of souls has sustained the apostolic courage of the disciples throughout the centuries. According to an ancient author Saint Paul knew for himself "the pain of childbirth for those who, through him, believed in the Lord up until Christ was formed in them. After all, does he not say: 'my little children, for whom I am again in the pain of childbirth until Christ is formed in you' (Gal 4:19) and 'in Christ Jesus I became your father (1 Cor 4:15).'"[187]

Thus our sufferings are a communion of suffering with Christ (cf. Rom 8:17); death is a communion of death with him (cf. 2 Tim 2:11). It is especially in his passion and death that Jesus became redemption (cf. 1 Cor 1:30). The Christian also becomes redemption with him: "Death is at work in us, but life in you" (2 Cor 4:12). Martyrdom would come and crown the apostle Peter: "Simon, son of John, do you love me?...Feed my lambs....Follow me" into death (cf. Jn 21:15–19). Jesus wanted the twelve to be with him (cf. Mk 3:14).

WITNESSES OF THE RISEN JESUS

Founded long ago, the Church must be constantly be refounded through an encounter of communion with the Risen One, just as it was in the beginning. For no person is Christian by birth—he or she must become one. It is necessary for the Church, the eschatological mystery, to take root unceasingly over the centuries in the midst of people.

How do we encounter the Risen One? He is elsewhere—neither visible, audible, nor tangible. Yet humans cannot know anything except through their senses, or at least, starting with the senses. So, in order to encounter him, Jesus comes under other appearances, in real symbols of his presence. He has created sacraments of encounter and of communion with him. While leaving his disciples in the world (cf. Jn 17:11), he makes them ascend to him, like the Twelve whom he called to climb the mountain with him (cf. Mk 3:13). Each one is "called to be an apostle" by "being set apart for the gospel" (Rom 1:1). That gospel was Christ himself in his saving mystery, and it propagates itself in the world through his disciples.

The disciples' role is to be "a witness...to his resurrection" (Acts 1:22). They do not witness merely to an event of the past, for a past event does not save people today and does not make new creatures of them. To simply transmit the testimony of the first disciples who saw the Risen One, and to recall former events is the work of a historian and not of "a witness...to his resurrection." The Church witnesses not only to a past event but to a person: "You will be my witnesses" (Acts 1:8). It bears witness to Jesus" (cf. Rev 1:2)[188] whom it encounters and experiences *today*: "We declare to you what we have seen and heard" (1 Jn 1:3). "And we have seen and do testify that the Father has sent his Son as the Savior of the world" (1 Jn 4:14).[189] The Church encounters Christ in his resurrection and it must witness to that. For it is in the resurrection that Jesus comes to the Church and makes himself known. The paschal mystery is linked to the second coming and creates witnesses that it needs for spreading news of that mystery in the world.

The Eucharist, the foremost sacrament of the coming of Christ to the Church, is the unparalleled sacrament of witness. The disciples at Emmaus recognized him during the breaking of the bread (cf. Lk 24:35) and announced the resurrection. At liturgy the faithful sing: "We proclaim your death, Lord Jesus, we celebrate your resurrection." They are witnesses of Jesus in his resurrection. Because Jesus lives forever in his resurrection,[190] it emerges most visibly in the world as the Eucharist. Partakers of the Eucharist can say to those who do not yet know: "Christ is risen. We have encountered him, we live from him."

But it is not enough for the Church to say what it knows in order to arouse faith. Faith does not merely accept facts that have been attested to or truths that have been taught by others. To believe is to put one's faith in someone. Faith receives Christ as nourishing bread (cf. Jn 6:26–47). It comes to Christ and clings to him (cf. Jn 7:37). Could a person attain faith if Christ did not come to encounter him or her, or if the holy bread were not offered? Faith is ignited by such an encounter. *To awaken faith, a witness must be a mediator of presence and encounter.*

Through his witnesses, Christ comes in person. Saint Augustine said: "Christ preaches Christ"[191]; again, "it is Christ—the Church who preaches Christ, the body preaches the head."[192] The gospel announces itself by its own dynamism, this gospel that is Christ in his Passover. The gospel is spread by the Church who is the body of Christ in his Passover: "The light bears witness to itself...is itself its own witness...so that the light may be known."[193] In the persons and the words of its witnesses, the Church is the illuminator of Christ. It is an epiphany of the paschal mystery. It mediates the encounter with Christ in the mystery of salvation.

No one can anoint him or herself a witness of the Risen One. No one can decide on their own to be a mediator of the coming of Christ or of an encounter with him, just as bread cannot itself become Eucharist. It is by the power of the Spirit that God raised Jesus and raises him today to be seen and heard in the world through apostles and their testimony.

TWO SACRAMENTS OF THE SECOND COMING

Christ makes himself visible and audible in the Church. The Church is itself a sacrament and makes available other means of salvation called "the sacraments." Through this sacrament of salvation,[194] people can enter into communion with Christ.

In juridical type theologies the question would be raised: "When and by what words did Jesus institute these sacraments?" They consider, for example, that baptism was instituted by Jesus' command: "Make disciples of all nations, baptizing them..." (Mt 28:19); the Eucharist by another directive: "Do this in remembrance of me" (Lk 22:19); and reconciliation by this one: "If you forgive the sins of any, they are forgiven" (Jn 20:23). Such theologies hold that Jesus, having obtained salvation for humankind by his merits, then instituted specific rites for applying those merits, like dispensing posts with officials in charge at each post. One word of institution was required, and it sufficed. And the Church today repeats those rites instituted so long ago.[195]

However, Jesus is the continuous event of salvation and its coming via the sacraments. The institution of several sacraments may be pointed to by certain passages of Scripture; but in his Passover, Christ himself is their endless institution. The sacraments are agents through which Christ comes to save us. They are the hands by which the paschal mystery draws people and gathers them together.

Two sacraments will be presented here: (1) the Word, where the general sacramentality of the Church is expressed; and (2) the Eucharist. One is a beginning, the other is the "summit of evangelization."[196] Both are real symbols of the paschal mystery and its second coming; of its emergence in the world and the means of communion with Christ.

THE SACRAMENT OF THE WORD

Jesus is the Word proclaimed in the world. God pronounced that word convincingly by raising Jesus. From then on that Word is heard through the activity of the Church, which is the sacrament of Christ in his resurrection and in his coming to the world. "It is Christ who lives in me," says Saint Paul (Gal 2:20); "Christ is speaking in me" (2 Cor 13:3). The basic activity of the Church in its various forms is to be the voice of the one who is the message of salvation (cf. Acts 13:26) in person. The proclamation of the gospel is an authentic sacrament, although it is not included with the other seven. Yet, the Church, as fundamental sacrament, is disclosed by the gospel's proclamation.

The word is not only a statement, it actually conveys the mystery it tells about: "When you received the word of God that you heard from us, you accepted it not as a human word but as what it really is, God's word, which is also at work in you believers" (1 Thess 2:13), and accomplishes what it proclaims.

Gospel is another name for the apostolic word. It brings about the salvation it proclaims: "Our message of the gospel came to you not in word only, but also in power and in the Holy Spirit and with full conviction" (1 Thess 1:5). It is "the power of God for salvation to everyone who has faith" (Rom 1:16). "Now I would remind you…of the good news…through which also you are being saved" (1 Cor 15:1–2). When Paul said that he was set apart for "the gospel of God,"[197] one can surmise that the gospel is the very mystery of salvation that enters the world in the form of proclamation. Paul was brought into and consecrated in this mystery[198] that spreads. One could say that the gospel is Jesus rising in the form of an apostle and preaching. Paul accomplished the gospel of Christ by the power of the Spirit (cf. Rom 15:19).[199] He not only proclaimed the Good News, he participated in its realization. He acknowledged "the commission…to make the word of God fully known, the mystery that has been hidden throughout the ages…Christ in you, the hope of glory" (Col 1:25–27). "Living and active," the Word produces the salvation that it proclaims (cf. Heb 4:12).

And that salvation is the forgiveness of sins (cf. Lk 1:77). According to the Synoptics, Jesus gave the command to "proclaim the good news to the whole creation" (Mk 16:15). According to John, he sent the disciples to forgive sins in the power of the Spirit: "'As the Father has sent me, so I send you.' When he had said this, he breathed on them and said to them, 'Receive the Holy Spirit. If you forgive the sins of any, they are forgiven them; and if you retain the sins of any, they are retained'" (Jn 20:21–23). At the beginning of the Johannine account, the Precursor declared: "Here is the Lamb of God, who takes away the sin of the world!" The Lamb is the one who "baptizes with the Holy Spirit" (Jn 1:29–33). At the apex of the account, Jesus was referred to once again as the Passover Lamb, none of whose bones would be broken (cf. Jn 19:36).

From his open side there flowed water, the Johannine symbol of the Holy Spirit (cf. 7:37–39). Having the Holy Spirit at his disposal from that point on, Jesus poured the Spirit out on his disciples and sent them to take away the sin of the world. The Gospel of John is framed between this beginning and this end that define it as the gospel of the paschal Lamb of God who, in the power of the Holy Spirit, takes away sin. Like Jesus, the disciples were sent in that power for the same goal. That is the Johannine account of sending the apostles. By evangelizing, they take away the sin of the world.

The power to forgive sins is limitless. Its totality is expressed by opposing the contraries: to forgive and to retain.[200] This power is divine since God alone can forgive sins (cf. Mk 2:7). The sinner destroys the bond of paternity and filiation that God had established. Who can reestablish it except God? Forgiveness requires begetting a person in the holiness of the Spirit with grace that transforms the sinner into a child of God. The Father takes the sinner into his Son begotten in the Holy Spirit, and who was raised in the same Spirit for our justification (cf. Rom 4:25). Such work is divine.

How do the disciples share in this divine activity?[201] The mission conferred is all-embracing: it is that of Jesus who takes away the sin of the world. Sent like him, the Church evangelizes the nations (cf. Mt 28:19); evangelizing them, it converts them and converting them, takes away their sins (cf. Lk 24:47–49). Forgiveness is a grace of conversion. Conversion results from the work of reconciliation (cf. 2 Cor 5:18–19). The Good News that is the mystery of Christ spreading himself out in the world forgives sins because it is disseminated and received. The faith that one receives and in which a person is justified, freed from sin, is the faith that "comes from what is heard, and what is heard comes through the word of Christ" (Rom 10:17). The forgiveness of sins is the fruit of the gospel.

The Church evangelizes in different ways: by the preached word, by the word expressed in sacramental symbols, and by the many testimonies of faith. The Church recognizes a specific sacrament of forgiveness, penance/reconciliation, whose goal is to re-Christianize or to Christianize the faithful more deeply, purifying them of sins committed after baptism. But sin is forgiven not as a debt that one cancels. Rather, the Church asks the sinner to convert and then brings his or her conversion about. The words of absolution are the outcome of the effective proclamation of the Good News in the Christian community, particularly during the celebration of that sacrament, which is truly another sacrament of evangelization.

To be in a position to forgive sins, or to be an agent of conversion, the Church must first itself receive the conversion-oriented power of the Risen One. The saying, "Receive the Holy Spirit" (cf. Jn 20:22), means that the Spirit is given. It also means that the Church must be open to that Spirit, and receive the Spirit for itself.[202]

THE EUCHARIST

The eucharistic celebration is the strongest word of salvation proclaimed through the ministry of the Church. It is the "summit of evangelization." The whole mystery that is communicated in the Good News is condensed into the Eucharist. Eucharist is the foremost paschal sacrament for it is inseparable from Christ's death and Resurrection, and from his presence as he comes into the world.

The second coming aspect of the Eucharist is fundamental. Christ made himself present, and the disciples recognized him. Jesus said: "This is my body" (Lk 22:19). For a Jew, "body" refers to the entire person. In Scripture, "blood poured out" refers to not only the liquid that flows throughout the body, but designates the entire person as a victim of violence (cf. Mt 26:28). Jesus referred to himself that way in the eucharistic formulas. He declared in John 6:51, 56: "I am the living bread....Those who eat my flesh and drink my blood abide in *me*." A disciple enters into communion with the whole person of Christ.

Jesus was given to the disciples immolated—body handed over and blood poured out—but also in glory. As a meal, the Eucharist is the symbol and source of life. It is called living bread (cf. Jn 6:51). According to Luke 22:15–20 it was instituted as "the Passover...fulfilled in the kingdom of God." It speaks of life in death. It is the paschal sacrament of Jesus, glorified in the death through which he was glorified for all eternity. It is "the Lord's supper" (1 Cor 11:20).

The Eucharist is sacrificial. Eucharist is the sacrament of death and resurrection, because it is the Body of Christ, which is the body handed over (cf. Mt 20:18). It is Christ coming to the Church where he is remembered forever in his death and resurrection.[203] Christ makes himself present at the moment when salvation is being realized, that is, when his body is being handed over and glorified, so that the Church may become a single body, bringing about salvation with him. The Eucharist is the sacrament of the presence of Christ, and is sacrificial because of his presence. Jesus died and was raised for all (cf. 2 Cor 5:15), coming to earth and giving himself through death and resurrection. Bread and wine manifest the "for us" aspect of his "coming and giving" because they are obviously intended *for* guests to be consumed.

From the very beginning Christians were aware that eating this bread and drinking this cup brought them into communion with the Lord (cf. 1 Cor 10:16–17). The meal was called "the table of the Lord" (1 Cor 10:21) and "the Lord's supper" (1 Cor 11:20). Previously, when anyone ate with Jesus, they knew they were also invited to a meal in the kingdom (cf. Mk 10:37).

But then Jesus died. Yet it was "in the breaking of the bread" after his death that one found Jesus again amid his own people. The Book of Revelation has borrowed from the eucharistic liturgy one of its most beautiful images: "Listen, I am standing at the door, knocking; if you hear my voice and open the door, I will come in to you and eat with you" (Rev 3:20).[204]

The word *parousia* means "presence" and "coming." Jesus makes himself present by being elsewhere, and by coming from that other place without leaving it. To be visible in this world, he makes use of realities in the world: bread and wine. His presence is thereby veiled, but it promises to be made known: "You proclaim the Lord's death until he comes" (1 Cor 11:26). The word *until* seems to express a finality, saying in other words, "so that he may come."[205] The desire is burning, *"Marana tha."* We can be certain of his coming because of his presence.

Coming from elsewhere without leaving it, Christ becomes present by drawing us to himself. He draws to himself the bread and the wine and then, by drawing them, he draws the faithful. Veiled, his presence does not exercise all its power to attract; otherwise the Church would cease to be earthly (cf. 1 Jn 3:2). As the sacrament of the heavenly meal, the Eucharist is for a Church that is "on its way."

Two gospels evoke the Eucharist in their accounts of Christ's post-resurrection appearances. Luke places the episode of the Emmaus disciples in a eucharistic framework. At first Jesus was not recognized. He began by introducing the disciples to a Christian interpretation of Scripture.[206] At table he repeated the gestures of the Last Supper. The disciples ate the offered bread and then recognized Jesus. Then they went to recount to the other disciples, "How he had been made known to them in the breaking of the bread" (Lk 24:35).[207]

According to the Gospel of John, the Risen One appeared twice, both times on Sundays, the Lord's Day (cf. Rev 1:10), the first and eighth day of the week, the day of the resurrection, and of the second coming. Everything happened, even though the doors were closed, just as it does in the Eucharist when Jesus comes, sacrificed and marked by the wounds of the passion, yet glorious, as well. A third time he "showed himself" on the shores of the Sea of Tiberias. Jesus stood on the shore at dawn. Could that not be the shore of eternity at the dawn of the Day that is proclaimed? The appearance was mysterious. Once Jesus was recognized, they still wanted to ask who he was (cf. Jn 21:12). Previously, in this same place, Jesus had offered the crowd the multiplied bread and fish—Johannine symbols of the Eucharist. That morning he likewise offered a loaf of bread and fish. The whole account strongly points to the Eucharist. The Eucharist is the sacrament through which Christ appears to us.

Theology asks itself the question: How is the Eucharist a sacrifice when it is a meal? How is Eucharist the presence of Christ, when the taste of bread and wine seem to be the only experience we get of them?[208] The answer is contained in the paschal mystery whose sacrament is the Eucharist.

To answer the first question, it used to be said that the priest immolates Christ. By means of the blade of his word he separates the body and the blood and thus renews in an unbloody way the sacrifice of the cross.[209] But the sacrifice of Christ is unique, and unrepeatable (cf. Heb 10:12–14). Jesus did not institute sacrificing priests—he abolished them. He established apostles whose mission is to bring people into communion with him in a uniquely redemptive sacrifice.

Modern theology no longer speaks of repeating the sacrifice. Instead, the Eucharist is understood as the sacrament of that one unique sacrifice. If we ignore the unity of Jesus' death and glorification, then we affirm that the Eucharist is merely a symbol of something in the past. Like looking in the rear-view mirror of a car, we view Christ's death as something that is behind us, as if it is a deed which has been completed once forever. But Jesus said: "This is my body, which is given for you...the cup that is poured out" (Lk 22:19–20). We cannot proclaim the real presence of Christ in the Eucharist without also admitting the reality of Christ's sacrifice. Christ is as much handed over to the Father as he is present on the altar. In the mystery of his obedient death, he was made eternal in glory.

The Eucharist does not reproduce that unique and unrepeatable sacrifice. Nor does it simply evoke a memory of some sacrifice from the past. It is the emergence of that sacrifice into today's world realities, making it accessible to us through communion. It is the paschal sacrament, not *post*-paschal. It is the unique Passover celebrated by Jesus and his disciples. "Each time we offer this memorial sacrifice, the work of our redemption is accomplished *(exercetur)*."[210]

The paschal mystery is hidden but the Eucharist makes it visible. Jesus said: "Where is my guest room where I may eat the Passover with my disciples?" (Mk 14:14). Today Christ brings us, his disciples, into the eternal celebration of the Passover of his death and Resurrection. The Eucharist is the sacrament of Christ's sacrifice because through the Eucharist Christ gives himself to us in his unique sacrifice, which was his death and resurrection, and through which he was made eternal. He gives himself to the Church so that we may celebrate with him that one unique sacrifice.

How does the Church celebrate the sacrifice? Not by repeating it—after all, it is unique. Not by completing it, for it is infinite. The Church offers the sacrifice by receiving it: "Take, eat" (Mt 26:26). That is the basic premise of the eucharistic celebration. Christ comes, and the Church receives. Christ comes in his sacrifice, and the Church receives him there. The Church offers by receiving, but it does not receive passively. The Church lets itself be grasped by Christ through his eucharistic second coming. It lets itself be incorporated into the redemptive sacrifice. By receiving Christ, the Church shares in his sacrifice. It celebrates his sacrifice by identifying with Christ in it.

The Eucharist is the body of Christ in that redemptive act. And it is given to the Church so that the Church may become what it receives: the body of Christ in his redemptive act. Saved this way in Christ and with him, the Church shares in the action of saving the world.

The other question is secondary. However, it is especially taxing to the intelligence of theologians.[211] How do bread and wine become the body and blood of Christ while they remain entirely unchanged in their appearances?

Two divergent lines of thought present themselves for reflection here. One takes as its point of departure the earthly realities (bread, wine, meal). The other begins with the mystery which those earthly realities represent in the sacrament.

Since the Middle Ages, theologians have been opting for the first: how can bread and wine be transformed into the body and blood of Christ? How can a meal become a sacrament of communion with Christ?

Scholastic theology uses the philosophy of Aristotle who separated every material reality into its "substance" and its "accidents." Accidents are external and variable characteristics such as quantity, quality, taste, shape, and so on. We know, for example, that bread can take on many different shapes and textures and still be bread. Wine can have different colors and tastes, but still be wine. The substance that is bread or wine receives its appearance to our senses from its accidents (that is, its accidental characteristics). Presuming this distinction between substance and accident is true, then God can, by his power, change the "substances" of bread and wine into those of his body and blood while keeping entirely the "accidents" of bread and wine.[212] To anyone who adheres to the philosophy of Aristotle this explanation demonstrates that faith in the eucharistic presence does not contradict reason.

But all of this is extraneous to the paschal mystery and, therefore, to the Eucharist that is its sacrament. It is also extraneous to the mystery of the Incarnation which is the foundation of all sacramentality, and whose summit is the paschal mystery.[213] In the Incarnation, the humanity of Jesus was incorporated into his divinity without losing any of his human richness. On the other hand, bread and wine in the above schema become the body and blood of Christ by ceasing to be bread and wine. The divine power at work there would allow the creator to transform any earthly substance into any other earthly substance regardless of its accidents. But we are dealing with Christ who is unique, and who is not just earthly. The power that transforms the eucharistic elements is also unique—it is the power that raised Jesus. It is the power of the Holy Spirit who gives Christ power to bring all things under subjection to himself and to transform them (cf. Phil 3:21). This theory proposed by scholastic theology does not understand the words *body* and *blood* in their biblical sense as Jesus intended them to mean: that his entire being was being handed over, and thus sacrificed. It also ignores the fact that Eucharist is a sacrament of sacrifice because, and to the extent that, it is the sacrament of Christ's presence. In the older theory Christ's presence is static—it is simply his body and blood sitting there. But the paschal mystery, whose sacrament is the Eucharist, is always linked to the second coming. The presence of Christ in his Passover is not only a substance, it is a person who comes, who invites, and who gives himself: "Take and eat. This is my body [me]...Poured out for [you]" (Mt 26:26–28). In its scholastic explanation the eucharistic transformation is a disjointed block in the Christian landscape not linked to the total mystery of the incarnate and saving Son of God. Thus the explanation is to be sought elsewhere.

In modern times other philosophies have replaced Aristotle. In reflecting on Eucharist, contemporary thought has become more personalist, and therefore closer to the paschal mystery and the second coming. But many theologians still look for keys to understanding this in earthly realities. They draw inspiration from the possibility that humans have to change one reality into another by giving it a new meaning. Instead of transubstantiation some speak of trans-signification. Here is an example. For a flock of animals the flowers of the meadow are plants for grazing. For the young man who gathers them and offers them to his fiancée, they are no longer plants for grazing, but a bouquet full of the meaning that love attributes to it. Or the glass of wine that two lovers drink, who perhaps are not thirsty except for each other, is a sign and realization of their communion. "Having loved his own, ...he loved them to the end" (Jn 13:1). Then he took bread and gave it to them. The bread was transformed while still remaining bread, and it became the sacrament of communion.

This illustration is interesting but its explanation remains inadequate. Transformation described this way is a justification. It is an incomplete description of communion between persons who remain separated. They come together in symbols that are devoid of themselves. But in order to be united, husbands and wives no longer resort to such symbols. In the Eucharist, Christ and the Church are married. Christ takes hold of the bread and wine to realize what two spouses want: a genuine communion in only one body. He does not *attribute* a new meaning to the bread, the wine, and the meal.[214] Rather, he *creates* their eucharistic meaning, which is the truth about their paschal and second coming, and he brings about their unity in only one body, his own. In this way the Eucharist prepares for the final resurrection (cf. Jn 6:58), which the theory of transsignification does not seem to explain.

The meal of bread and wine make visible the sacramental body and blood of Christ, but they do not explain how they became his body and blood. To understand, we must look to Christ who, in his paschal mystery, makes the bread and wine his sacrament. The key to understanding is in the symbolism of a house where the door opens only from the inside. The paschal mystery itself includes his coming and his eucharistic presence, for by its nature it is linked to Christ's second coming.

How is Christ present in this world and how can he make his presence visible? God is present by reason of his creative omnipresence. Christ is present in the Incarnation that is itself redemptive. The Father is present without being part of creation. Christ is in the world and belongs to the world. How is he in this world? Not like other creatures. He is present everywhere because he is the pinnacle of creation, and is where everything begins and toward which everything has been created. "He is... the firstborn of all creation...all things have been created through him and for him...and in him all things hold together" (Col 1:15–17). He is present in the world because he is its Alpha and Omega. As such, he acts on the world through the power of the Spirit which makes him Lord of all: "By the power...to make all things subject to himself" (Phil 3:21).

If Christ wishes to manifest more greatly his presence in the world, that is, if he wishes to make bread, wine, and the assembly of the faithful into sacraments of a more intense presence— even a total presence—then he acts on those creatures by increasing his presence in them since they are already created through him and for him and already exist in him. *He takes greater hold of what already belongs to him, re-creating these realities even more strongly toward himself.*

He does not enter them from the outside, for he is already present in them. He does not come down from heaven, he does not leave that other place where he is, and he does not exit from the world of eternity where he is. Rather, he comes to the world by drawing to himself the bread, wine, and the faithful. He does not take away from the bread and wine, or the faithful their proper existence leaving only their appearances or "accidents."[215] His role as our fullness is not to change, abolish, or to empty us. His role is to fill us up, to increase his own being in us. Bread and wine thus become true food and drink (cf. Jn 6:55). Whoever avails him or herself of them will never die because the life of the resurrection has begun (cf. Jn 6:50–58). While still "fruit of the earth and the work of human hands," this bread has also become the bread of eternal life.

The liturgy uses the proper language when it speaks of sanctification, and of consecration of the offerings. How does God sanctify earthly realities? God does so through the power of the Holy Spirit, by which Christ is glorified and made the most profound substance of the world. God transforms the bread and the wine *by enriching their being. He enriches them by re-creating them. He re-creates them by drawing them to a closer relationship with him, indeed a relationship of oneness with him. He is their ultimate fullness: the Christ in whom "all things hold together"* (Col 1:17). Earthly bread becomes *eschatological bread.* It becomes a meal of heavenly communion with Christ who died and was raised. Just as a person's body is the visible part of that person, so the consecrated bread becomes the eucharistic body of Christ. The visible part of his presence on earth comes to the pilgrim Church so that it is rooted in its ultimate fullness.

The Eucharist is only one of the elements (but a central one) of the sacramental instruments inaugurated by Christ's Resurrection. The Church itself is Christ's body. It is the sacrament of Christ's paschal presence. The Church's relation to the Eucharist is evident, and the first centuries paid it great attention.

Irenaeus wrote: "Just as the bread that comes from the earth, after having received the invocation of God, is no longer ordinary bread, but the Eucharist, made of two things, the one earthly, the other heavenly, so our bodies that share in the Eucharist are no longer corruptible, because they have experienced the resurrection."[216]

Faustus, bishop of Riez (died c. A.D. 500), is explicit: "Ask yourself, you who are already regenerated by Christ....Why should it appear unheard of and impossible to you that earthly and mortal elements are transformed into the substance of Christ?...Externally you have received nothing in addition, internally you have changed everything....Likewise when you go up to the venerable altar to satisfy your hunger there, look in faith at the sacred body and blood of your God...One cannot doubt that these primary creatures (the bread and wine) can, at the order of his Power...be changed in their essence to become the body of Christ, when one sees humans themselves become the body of Christ by the work of his divine mercy."[217]

The Church and the Eucharist bear the same name: body of Christ. (Both constitute the New *Diathēkē* Covenant): "The cup...is the new covenant in my blood" (Lk 22:20; 1 Cor 11:25). That "New Covenant" is also "Jerusalem...our mother" (cf. Gal 4:24–26), who is the Church in its mystery. By the same power of the Spirit, Jesus rose and now rises visibly in the form of the Church and the Eucharist.

God makes humans the body of Christ by calling them to a new relationship with Christ, making them exist even more in him "through whom and for whom" they were created. Human beings are not stripped of their basic humanity, and no human characteristics are altered. But everything is elevated and consecrated into a new relationship of oneness with Christ. From now on human beings are in Christ Jesus. Christ lived in Paul without Paul ceasing to be himself: "Christ who lives in me...I live by faith in the Son of God" (Gal 2:20). It is the same with the bread and wine. They are consecrated into a relationship of oneness with Christ in his Passover. They become totally eschatologized.[218]

Numerous other analogies may help cast some light on this. Everything in Christianity speaks of a salvation that changes nothing and leads to fullness. Jesus did not abolish the law and the prophets—he brought them to fulfillment (cf. Mt 5:17). The words of Jesus (cf. Jn 14:24) and those of Paul are the word of God without ceasing to be words of Jesus and Paul. The principle is universal: grace does not destroy nature, it elevates it.

The mystery of the Incarnation offers the most illuminating analogy. During the earthly life of Jesus, people saw in him an authentic human being, and they were not mistaken. Our human experience sees in the Eucharist true bread and true wine. It cannot be mistaken, either. Jesus was a man but he was divinely consecrated (cf. Jn 10:26). The Eucharist consists of bread and wine, but consecrated by the Holy Spirit in Christ. Peter saw the earthly man *and* the Son of God; Christians see bread and wine *and* the real presence of Christ. For the Fathers of the eastern Church, the mystery of the Incarnation was the model for understanding eucharistic transformation. Toward the middle of the second century, Saint Justin wrote: "But just as Jesus Christ our Savior was made flesh through the word of God and took on flesh and blood for our salvation...so too the food over which the Eucharist has been spoken becomes the flesh and blood of the incarnate Jesus. Thus we have been taught."[219]

So the Incarnation offers not merely an analogy. Having reached its paschal summit, the Incarnation realizes the Eucharist.[220]

Chapter Nine

PASCHAL MYSTERY
AND CREATION

C hristian thought has always been strictly monotheistic. Very early, however, it acknowledged Christ as having a divine role in creation. That follows from belief in Jesus as the one who was raised in omnipotence, seated at the right hand of God. The disciples knew that God employed the utmost of "what is the immeasurable greatness of his power ...God put this power to work in Christ, when he raised him from the dead and seated him at his right hand in the heavenly places...above every name that is named" (Eph 1:19–21). The name "Lord" granted to Jesus (cf. Phil 2:9–10) is God's name in his creative omnipotence. As head of all, Christ exercises a power that stretched to the foundations of the world (cf. Eph 1:22).

"EVERYTHING IS CREATED IN HIM"

God is Father and in everything he acts as such.[221] If God creates, he does so in relationship to the Son at the very heart of the mystery of paternity and filiation: "All things came into being through him (the Son) and without him not one thing came in to being" (Jn 1:3). Does the prologue of John's gospel pose a question about the Son as considered apart from the Incarnation or apart from Jesus Christ? One can debate the issue. In any case, in Paul it is Christ Jesus, the Incarnate Word, who is the mediator of creation: "There is one God, the Father, from whom are all things and for whom we exist, and one Lord, Jesus Christ, through whom are all things and through whom we exist" (1 Cor 8:6). The hymn in Colossians 1:15–20 talks about Christ Jesus: "In him all things in heaven and on earth were created...through him and for him. He himself is before all things, and in him all things hold together." As firstborn of all creation, he also belongs to creation, and everything is transcendent in him (cf. Col 1:15). According to Revelation 3:14, Jesus is "the origin of God's creation."

But can one attribute that role to Christ Jesus and proclaim that he "is before all things, and in him all things hold together" (Col 1:17), even though he entered history late? To say "yes" is not a contradiction because it deals with the Christ of glory. It is about the "Lord"; hence, the glorified Jesus that Paul declares: "From whom are all things" (1 Cor 8:6). It is in the glorified Christ that Paul sees God in whose image everything was created (cf. 2 Cor 4:4). "The firstborn of all creation" is identical to "the firstborn from the dead" (cf. Col 1:15, 18).

The Lord Jesus Christ (cf. Phil 2:11) is seated at the right hand of God.[222] He shares the omnipotence of his Father who creates everything that is. Nothing contradicts the statement: "He himself is before all things" (Col 1:17), because in his glorification Jesus was appropriated entirely into that eternal instant when the Son was begotten. God raised him by saying: "You are my Son, today I have begotten you" (Acts 13:33). The instant in which he was appropriated is an eternal instant. It was before all things, and is at the beginning of all things. The fact that Jesus Christ existed before the world is not a temporal problem—it is primeval because creation began by begetting the Son into the world. God always creates in relationship to his Son; God also creates by the power of the Holy Spirit in which he begot the Son. Creation has its origin in the Trinity which Jesus is part of. Creation had a beginning. In its origin, however, it is eternal. Creation's beginning is in Christ, and in Christ's begetting by the Father at this current moment.

If everything is created in Christ, we can believe that from its beginning creation has a place in the glory of Christ. Yes, as a human Christ was created. But as Man/Son of God, he was begotten by God. Thus he is created and begotten. God's act of raising Jesus is very mysterious, for it was an act of begetting and of creating at the same time. God creates-begets this man, Jesus, *ex nihilo*, at the moment of death which reduces the human being to nothingness. Yet God also creates-begets him *ex plenitudine*—by the infinite overflowing of his paternal being.

The same is true for human beings, but at their level. They are not first created and subsequently adopted. From their origin they enjoy an existence in some relational way, already linked to the great relational mystery to which God has destined them, namely, resurrection in Jesus Christ.

The Holy Spirit is the power through which God creates-begets his Son in the world (cf. Lk 1:35) and leads him through earthly life and death to his glorious filial fullness (cf. Rom 8:11). The Holy Spirit was also the one who swept over the primordial waters (cf. Gen 1:2). It is the breath of life: "When you send forth your spirit, they are created; and you renew the face of the ground" (Ps 104:30).[223] This creator Spirit is the power of divine generation[224]—thus, the human person is a filial creature. As a filial being, each person receives him or herself from another. Each person is formed by opening the self and by receiving just as did Christ when he opened himself up completely to his Father in death. The human person is an open being who becomes his or her true self by their openness to receive from

God life, grace, and power. Any definition of the human person must include this relational aspect.

The Holy Spirit is "God's love" (cf. Rom 5:5). God raised Jesus in the Holy Spirit. He raised him by loving him, making him "a spirit of power and of love" (cf. 2 Tim 1:7). God creates-begets humans by loving them in his Son, as Saint Thomas Aquinas said, "The key of love having opened his hand, he brought out creatures from it."[225] Since it was created in Christ and the Spirit, creation is strewn with seeds of love, and therefore all humans are children of God: "Everyone who loves is born of God" (1 Jn 4:7).

The human person has been described as a being created for death. But the human person has also been created for resurrection. According to the plan of creation each person is destined to die with Christ whom the Father raised. Thus the human person is immortal, not exempt from death, but created also to rise through death.[226]

Because God creates all people in Christ, who is the image of the invisible God, a divine reflection settles on each person's face. Jesus' saying, "Whoever sees me sees him who sent me" (Jn 12:45) applies at least partially to the human person and to the relationship found in all of creation: "Ever since the creation of the world his [God's] eternal power and his divine nature, invisible though they are, have been understood and seen through the things he has made" (Rom 1:20). Humans discover God far better by a simple look at the world than by the steep paths of logic. Such a look serves as a prelude to faith whose eyes penetrate the intimate mystery of God. Creation is the first Sacred Scripture written by God through the Holy Spirit and offered to all people to read. Jesus Christ, through whom and for whom everything is created, is the greatest Sacred Scripture. In that sense Christianity is a religion of the book.[227]

"EVERYTHING IS CREATED TOWARD HIM"[228]

The fullness of Christ is the source from which everything flows and the summit toward which everything converges. God creates by making his Son the point of departure and by attracting everything back toward him.

The image of God creating things by drawing them toward himself is familiar to us. "God…calls into existence the things that do not exist" (Rom 4:17).[229] We can imagine all of creation as a call that derives created things from the fullness of Christ and draws them back toward it. All creation is rooted in the dynamic fullness of Christ and is powerfully drawn toward him. Christ in glory is the alpha point of creation through being its omega point. The lordship of Christ "lifted up from the earth" (Jn 12:32) is made evident because creation is attracted to him.

Thus created, the world exists peacefully on its way. True, the so-called fleshly realities in history precede those that are spiritual. "But it is not the spiritual that is first, but the natural and then the spiritual" (1 Cor 15:46). The first announces the other: "If there is a physical body, there is also a spiritual body" (1 Cor 15:44). Sacred history goes from "the flesh" to "the spirit," that is, to the heavenly reality that is the Christ of glory. Institutions in the Old Testament were merely a shadow of that idea: "These are only a shadow of what is to come; but the substance [that causes the shadow] belongs to Christ" (Col 2:17).

Creation evolved by degrees in a passive manner up until the introduction of humans with their dignity as relational persons. Humans have since then ascended toward Christ in their loving obedient relationship to God. But humanity has not yet attained perfect obedience. According to Saint Irenaeus, Adam was still only a child in humanity.[230] The happy couple put in paradise at the beginning of the biblical account means that God's work is good: "God saw everything that he had made, and indeed it was very good" (Gen 1:31). But the real paradise was not the one present at the beginning. In the eyes of Saint Paul, Adam is the earthly man, created in imperfection, incapable of transmitting true life—he was a simple living being (cf. Gen 2:7). Perfection comes at the end in the last Adam who became a life-giving spirit (cf. 1 Cor 15:45). The real paradise can be found where creation begins and ends: "In the heavenly places, in Christ Jesus" (Eph 2:6). Jesus shared it with the good thief: "Today you will be with me in Paradise" (Lk 23:43). In Christ resides the original justice for which humanity was created. In his death, which is full of eternal life, humans possess immortality. "The last Adam," the ultimate ancestor, is the real one. Humans have descended from him through their attraction toward him. In converging toward Christ who is the origin, the human race finds its principle of unity better than it can from an earthly ancestor who, in begetting them, disperses his descendants.

The power that draws us toward final perfection is the very same power that achieves ultimate perfection in Christ. It is the creator Spirit and the Spirit of divine filiation through whom Jesus rose to filial fullness. The Spirit acts in the world as the power of "filialization"; "we ourselves, who have the first fruits of the Spirit, groan inwardly while we wait for adoption, the redemption of our bodies" (Rom 8:23). The Spirit of love draws all in love toward the Son who was begotten in love. Saint Augustine has said, "Our cornerstone is placed in the heavens to draw us toward it by the weight of charity."[231]

CREATION AND REDEMPTION, ONE WORK

According to a theology that was very widespread not long ago, creation and redemption constituted two distinct, successive works. God created, sin spoiled his work, then God devised a new plan that rectified the first, but only better. But if God creates in his Son, who is essentially the savior, all his work is therefore both creative and redemptive. The plan of God as presented in Ephesians 1:1–10 is both cosmic and salvific. God's plan is also unique according to Hebrews 2:10. "It was fitting that God, for whom and through whom all things exist, in bringing many children to glory, should make the pioneer of their salvation perfect through sufferings." Creation and the path to salvation are inseparable. To lead to glory is to lead creation to its completion.[232]

Belief in the salvific lordship of Christ leads to Christ's cosmic role. Lordship is God's (cf. Phil 2:9–11), and it is absolute. It belongs to a creator God. The first Christians to use cosmological language borrowed it from the theology of redemption.[233] In addition, we see that this was also the result of the saving interventions by God as he led Israel, also, to believe in an all-powerful Creator-God.

God has only one plan, and from its very beginning it is directed dynamically toward salvation. The act of creation is already salvific, because it is integrated into the mystery of redemption through the begetting of the Son into the world by the power of the Holy Spirit. In effect, humanity, which is anchored in the mystery of Christ's redemption, is created in him, who has been glorified in his death for us.

From the human perspective, creation and redemption succeed each other. That seems true especially as a need for redemption presupposes that humans fell into sin after their creation. But a prophetic approach to faith seeks to understand the whole divine order. Such faith begins with the fullness of Christ, from whom everything derives its source: "God has blessed us in Christ with every spiritual blessing in the heavenly places, just as he chose us in Christ, before the foundation of the world" (Eph 1:3–4). The "lamb without defect or blemish," although only "revealed at the end of the ages," was already "destined before the foundation of the world" (cf. 1 Pet 1:19–20).

If that is the case, then by creation humans are destined for salvation. They were not created sinners. After all, the work of God is good…could God create sinners? In every human being there is a link to Christ, a filial connection from the very beginning. Sin entered history upon a foundation of grace and it continues so in the life of every human being. Grace is even more original than sin.[234] God is holy and he is the Father. He creates children, not sinners. Humanity descends more profoundly from the coming Christ than it has from the sinner Adam, in whom it was not created. The universal salvific will of God was prescribed in the act of creation. Yet God's salvific will also appeals to humans for collaboration so that they will open themselves to being created by God and saved from their sins.

In a theology that distinguishes two successive actions—creation (spoiled by sin) and redemption—humans must first enter the path of salvation in order to be saved, because they were not born on it. They do so through faith and baptism. Whoever does not do so, remains excluded from salvation.[235] If, on the contrary, the plan of God is unified, and if humanity is created in Christ and for him, then it is already being saved through its birth. Humanity thus benefits from the link between Christ, the Church, and salvation.[236] In this system, the initiative by our saving God is obvious, and the gratuitousness of God's grace is total. This means that humans have already been called to salvation, even before they have sought it. And they lose salvation only if they refuse it.[237]

Humans refuse salvation if they do not let themselves be drawn toward Christ, who is salvation. They then abandon the path of salvation, which is meant to be creation's future, and is fulfilled through an attraction to communion with the Son. Humanity—children of God by creation—must still let itself be filialized by the creator. Despite the weight of sin that has been weighing on humanity from its beginning (cf. Rom 5:3–5), humanity must climb to its highest internal calling and participate in the creative act that draws it to the fullness of Christ in his death, and which returns fallen humanity to its original innocence. Humans are saved both by creation and in death to themselves when they fully accept their condition as loving obedient creatures the way God created them.

Death, therefore, is inevitable, for total death is inherent in Christ glorified, who is creation's ultimate fullness. But it is a death like Christ's, who died begotten in the filial embrace of God's creative paternity. For people who close themselves off from Christ, death is a sign of a curse (cf. Gen 2:17). But for those in communion with Christ, it is the moment of filial embrace. Death is an enemy of the human race: "Through the devil's envy / death entered the world, / and those who belong to his company experience it" (Wis 2:24). But they alone! By conforming to the plan of creation, death is the opposite of what it appears to be. It is really a sign of the glorious cross traced on humanity. Saint Irenaeus said that the Word of God "was inscribed in the form of a cross in creation....He became flesh and was stretched out on the wood to recapitulate everything in himself."[238] Christ, in whom and for whom humans are created, is "Jesus our Lord...handed over to death for our trespasses and was raised for our justification" (Rom 4:24-25). He is the original creature, firstborn of creation, the model for humanity.

Salvation is thus an entirely gratuitous act. It is not granted for a price paid to reconcile divine justice, nor is it granted to humans in order to let themselves be reconciled (cf. 2 Cor 5:19–20). Notice that forgiveness preceded the return of the Prodigal Son. It preceded even his sin. Forgiveness is contained in the paternal-creative action operating in Christ the savior. Forgiveness is freely given, and to be given, it asks only to be received. It is not merely a wiping away of sin. It is not God simply forgetting what was done and promising not to take into account our

offenses. Rather, it is part of creation itself, part of the genera-
tive process. It heals humans from their mortal wounds by giving them power to be born as children of God.

Up to their final moments of life on earth, humans can hope.
God is God for them in his immolated Son. God placed Christ at
the foundation of his work so that creation would be successful
and so that the world would be saved: "God so loved the world
that he gave his only Son" (Jn 3:16). In the sacrificed Son the
Father is also offered, for the Father is in the Son (cf. Jn 14:11).
The omnipotent God is all-powerful, for the sake of the world,
in his Son who died for it. In contemplating the mystery of the
redemptive Incarnation, John was able to say: "God is love" (1 Jn
4:8). He is for the world,

Chapter Ten

CREATION AT ITS COMPLETION

Whatever God begins, he brings to completion: "God is faithful" (1 Cor 1:9). He brings creation to its completion even in death, where one would think that all human hope has been dashed. God does for humanity just as he did for his Son, Jesus Christ.

HUMANITY IN ITS DEATH

Humanity is born to die. But its death is not the one spoken about in the Book of Genesis: "In the day that you eat of it you shall die" (2:17). "God did not make death... / he created all things so that they might exist" (Wis 1:13–14). God has a horror of the kind of death that ends life and breaks relationships—what we call mortal death. God's horror of death is as strong as his horror of sin, which results in death.

If humanity is created for death, then death must be something other than what it seems. God is creator as father in relationship to his Son. He creates in the Holy Spirit who is the power to beget. But a father does not beget only to kill. The Holy Spirit is love. Whoever loves says to others: "You must not die, I love you forever." If created humanity is mortal, then in God's plan death can only be at the service of humanity's birth as children of God.

The demon who is the force of destruction, "a murderer from the beginning" (Jn 8:44), has perverted the meaning of death. Jesus restored death's original dignity. He lived it in an exemplary way—in loving obedient relationship to the Father. As mediator of both creation and redemption, Jesus saves humanity by saving them from their death and by enabling them to die toward the Father in communion with himself.

In his paschal mystery, Jesus is the point of convergence for mortal humanity. Humanity is created toward him: "Jesus was about to die...to gather into one the dispersed children of God" (Jn 11:51–52). Many begin to unite themselves to Christ from the beginning of their lives on earth through baptism, and prepare themselves for the ultimate encounter with him in death. But all humanity is created mortal and is created toward Christ. All are destined to die Christ's obediently relational death with him.

The Church bears witness to the different ways it encounters Christ in death. It speaks of a particular judgment pronounced by him at the death of each person—he comes, therefore, to each person in death. The Church used to say a great deal about Jesus' descent into hell, that is, of his encounter with those who were not able to encounter him while they were alive. Without that encounter no one could enter the kingdom.

Christ, who is the kingdom, is also its way: "No one comes to the Father except through me" (Jn 14:6). He is the gate—whoever enters through him is saved (cf. Jn 10:9). "Christ is our Passover" (1 Cor 5:7) [NAB], both the passage and the means of passage. The human person, reduced to nothing in death, would not know how to raise him or herself up to God on mere earthly strength. Christ grants "entrance into the sanctuary" and places each person on "the new and living way that he opened for us through the curtain [that is, his flesh]" (Heb 10:19–20). The immolated shepherd takes the sheep on his shoulders. Christ comes to us while he is still elsewhere, standing on the shore of eternity. He comes to us by drawing us to himself—he always comes in that way. He attracts us by revealing himself—he always attracts in that way. He is truth and its splendor, its beauty and its sweetness. These are things that the human person loves. Jesus was transformed by the Spirit of love. Now we have the joy of being loved. Can anyone resist such a great attraction? At the moment of the gravest peril, reduced to total impotence, can a person refuse their savior, indeed such a loving savior? In creating humanity both for death and for a death that gives birth, God charges the moment of death with crowning graces.

We die of sickness or of some other physical cause. We die spiritually through Jesus Christ. It is Christ who makes us die toward the Father.[239] "For since we believe that Jesus died and rose again, even so, through Jesus, God will bring with him those who have died" (1 Thess 4:14).[240] Jesus has become the good death, just as he became redemption. He is in a position to take our death into his own dying toward the Father, so that we may live in him.

Death is very individual and it cannot be shared. However, Jesus has incorporated all humanity into himself (in whom and toward whom human beings have been created), and he has saved them in their own deaths by sharing his death with them. His sharing is immense and infinitely open. It is a sharing of the Son of God, who goes to the Father through the limitless power of the Holy Spirit, and is an infinite source that can draw us human beings into eternity. Christ thus completes what was begun in baptism: uniting humanity into a single body in the same Spirit (cf. 1 Cor 12:12–13) and into the same death (cf. Rom 6:3).

Paul spoke about a communion of death in baptism, but in his Second Letter to Timothy, he describes a communion of death at the end of life: "This saying is sure: / If we have died with him, we will also live with him" (2:11). Being joined in a single death is a more intimate and more intense communion than love can ever imagine. Saint Paul ardently longs for it: "For to me, living is Christ and dying is gain...my desire is to depart and be with Christ" (Phil 1:21–23).[241]

Communion with Christ is eternal. No separation is ever to be feared again, because we no longer have to cling and so there is no danger of losing hold. It is an eternal communion in death, which forms part of the heavenly life for us and for Christ. Communion with Christ is a door that is always open and which allows those who have died to dwell in heaven. They are immortal because of their communion with the Passover of Christ through death.

A PURIFYING JUDGMENT

In raising Christ, God appointed Jesus "as judge of the living and the dead" (Acts 10:42). In his Passover, Christ is the judgment God pronounces on the world: "Now is the judgment on this world" (Jn 12:31). This judgment was pronounced forever in Jesus who has been made eternal through his Passover.

Catholic tradition believes in a particular judgment that Christ pronounces on each person entering eternity. Knowing who the judge is and what his justice is, we can guess what particular judgment is.

God's justice, as revealed in Scripture, is God's holiness that has promulgated its law of love. It is transcendent, dependent only on itself, subject to neither merits nor sins,[242] and supremely gratuitous: "God says...: 'I will have mercy on whom I have mercy....' So it depends not on human will or exertion, but on

God who shows mercy" (Rom 9:14–16). God's justice is exercised by communicating itself. It justifies and sanctifies whoever opens him or herself to it (cf. Rom 3:23–25). God judges through the Spirit [243] who is divine holiness in person. The Spirit is love (cf. Rom 5:5). Judgment is a work of love. God judges by loving.

Jesus is the mediator of justice. He judges through his death and resurrection. He judges by sharing the justice in which he was glorified (cf. 1 Tim 3:16). In rising, he did not leave the mystery of his death; rather he became eternal in it.[244] He encounters each dying person and judges them in his own death. He is the advocate (cf. 1 Jn 2:1) of the one he is judging, their intercessor before God.[245] In the final encounter with each person, Christ exercises his justice by purifying them in his blood if the person consents to it. To see oneself judged like that must be a moment of great happiness and supreme deliverance: "God did not send the Son into the world to condemn the world, but in order that the world might be saved through him" (Jn 3:17).

The Catholic Church believes in a "plenary indulgence" that God grants at death called purgatory. God judges through Jesus Christ by a purifying and sanctifying pardon. Particular judgment and purgatory are two names for the same merciful action of God in Christ the Redeemer.

In the past we raised the questions: Where is purgatory, if heaven is above and hell below? and what is the fire that purifies the souls? A theology of the paschal mystery can answer both. The place of purgatory is Christ, its fire is the Holy Spirit. In his Passover, Jesus is the crucible of purification (cf. Rev 7:14). The Spirit of love purifies us by making us spiritually capable of love.

Purification involves suffering. Jesus, in his limited earthly existence, suffered to obtain the Father's unlimited glory. "He learned obedience through what he suffered; and having been made perfect…" (Heb 5:8–9). To free oneself of impurities, the sinner must pass through a painful fire. The suffering must be very great and the joy of burning in the fire of the Spirit must be very great, yet without diminishing the suffering.

We can think of purgatory as a time of dying toward the Father. It is a time different from time on earth, and we really have no concept of it.

In charity the Church invites us to come to the aid of the dead. Each person dies alone, on a distant shore, separated from friends and relatives by the distance that stretches between life and death. But Christian friendship is not broken and made helpless when a brother or sister needs it. The Spirit forms a bond of friendship stronger than death. Christ is the savior of every person, and of their friendships. The Church teaches that among the various means of praying for the dead the best is celebrating the Eucharist.[246] According to earthly time it is celebrated after death. But it is *in* death that the community rejoins the dead person. Those who share the Eucharist unite themselves to Christ in his Passover, beyond the barriers of earthly time. They rejoin him in his glorifying death at exactly the moment when Christ meets a person in death, judges and purifies them. A funeral Mass is a meal that gathers together Christ in his glorifying death, the dead person, and all his or her friends still on earth, all at the same table. It is a concelebration of the Passover of Christ.

The dead person dies in Christ and in the arms of friends. We can, therefore, be certain that we do not die alone. Every great Christian act is celebrated in Church: baptism, Eucharist, penance, marriage….Would that not also be true of the supreme act? A person dies in Christ and in the Church—the Church of earth and of heaven as it is united into one single body in communion with the glorifying death of Christ.

THE FINAL RESURRECTION

The judgment given at the moment of death sets the stage and is a preparation for the announcement of the general judgment God will make at the final resurrection. The question is raised: Would not what happens in death also set the stage and prepare the announcement of the final resurrection? The two theologies oppose each other on this point, consistent with their two ways of understanding the human person.

One can consider the human person as a being composed of a corruptible body and a spiritual soul. At death this composite is broken: the body decays and all that survives is "the separated soul." In this notion there is no concept of communion with Christ in his death and resurrection. Death breaks apart the human person and that is all. It reduces a person to a condition contrary to human nature by making them a separated soul.[247] This may lead us to think that death is merely an evil consequence of Adam's sin and that there is no distinction between the death of a sinner and the death of the just. We would then have to conclude that Christ did not really save humanity from death, which is the most basic result incurred by its condemnation (cf. Gen 2:17). Yet Paul declared that Christ has made even better what sin had spoiled (cf. Rom 5:12–20).

Another way to understand the human person according to biblical thought presumes an undivided unity of the person. A human being is a person who is corporeal. The whole person thus undergoes death. However, the person is also immortal because of his or her personal relationship with God.[248] In responding to those who denied the resurrection, Jesus pointed to the relationships entered into by God with Abraham, Isaac, and with Jacob. He entered into a covenant with them and will never repudiate it. To God all of them are alive (cf. Lk 20:37–38). The disciples of Jesus would live as well, because it is said of them: "And this is the will of him who sent me, that I should lose nothing of all that he has given me, but raise it up on the last day (Jn 6:39). He repeats it in John 11:25–26: "I am the resurrection and the life. Those who believe in me, even though they die, will live, and everyone who lives and believes in me will never die." Christ lives in all the faithful as the Risen One (cf. Gal 2:20). Could anyone then perish? Jesus "died and lived again so that he might be Lord of both the dead and the living" (Rom 14:9). Our immortality comes from our relationship with God.

As corporeal beings we die, and that changes our mode of existence. Jesus affirmed the resurrection by showing that Abraham, Isaac, and Jacob are alive. Saint Paul knew of only one life for the faithful in the hereafter: resurrection: "For if the dead are not raised, then Christ has not been raised...Then those also who have died in Christ have perished" (1 Cor 15:16, 18). The apostle knew that through death he would rejoin Christ: "My desire is to depart and be with Christ" (Phil 1:23). Paul trusted that he would rejoin Christ with his whole being. "...if the earthly tent we live in is destroyed, we have a building from God" (2 Cor 5:1).

We are saved from death, our enemy, together with Christ because the Father "was able to save him from death" (Heb 5:7). The Father had begotten Jesus in the world and did not permit that he perish as a man, which is the way he begot him. Through death the Father brought Jesus into fullness: "It was impossible for him to be held in its [death's] power....He was not abandoned to Hades" (Acts 2:24, 31). Jesus' survival is attributed, not to the immateriality of the soul, but to his relationship with God. Jesus was raised because of his filial relationship.

Paul made the distinction between our outer nature and our inner nature. One wastes away, the other is renewed day by day, undertaking an "eternal weight of glory," and, "what can be seen is temporary but what cannot be seen is eternal" (2 Cor 4:16–18). The human person passes from earth to heavenly existence in the depth of his or her being. What is this inner self? Created in the image of the God of mystery, the human person, too, is a mystery. Beyond what is visible in this person, the unknown is a child of God who must be born through death.

If we presume that everything is created in Christ and toward him, and that all things hold together in him, then can we not say that all humanity has an inner, universal self? Saint Paul felt "alive" in Christ: "I have been crucified with Christ…it is Christ who lives in me" (Gal 2:19–20). He also referred to life in Christ (cf. 1 Cor 1:30). Reversing the image, he talked of clothing oneself with Christ (cf. Gal 3:27). In John's gospel, Jesus uses two images: "You will know that…you [are] in me, and I in you" (Jn 14:20). When death comes, does not the person descend more deeply toward the interior of humanity that is Christ? Jesus said: "I am…the life" (Jn 11:25).[249] Thérèse of Lisieux, his faithful follower, declared: "I do not die, I enter into life."[250] Paul spoke of a heavenly dwelling that he would put on (cf. 2 Cor 5:1–4).[251] Yet already on earth he had put on Christ.

The final resurrection is not entirely unprecedented or without previous stages that have prepared for it. God does not create a person in the unity of body and soul, destining it to break apart and let the soul survive alone, and then to join the unity together again after a multi-millennial wait. God does not proceed in fits and starts. The Christian knows him or herself through Christ, raised in Christ's death, for which we have been created. If our death is our *dies natalis* (our day of birth), then death does not fragment our being. The sacraments that prepare the way are steps toward a progressive resurrection. Thus death becomes resurrection's most decisive stage.

From the beginning the Church has believed in a supreme salvific manifestation of Christ: "We wait for the blessed hope and the manifestation of the glory of our great God and savior, Jesus Christ" (Titus 2:13); also, "we are expecting a savior, the Lord Jesus Christ" (Phil 3:20).[252] The Church on earth awaits a future salvation. But even in the death of its members, it does not attain its complete perfection. The *dies natalis* of each one is not the high point of humanity. The Church is not a collection of people where each one is saved by him or herself. It is a community in which "we do not live to ourselves, and we do not die to ourselves" (Rom 14:7). Everyone is sanctified in the fabric of a common holiness. As long as the fabric is not yet fully woven, no saint has attained perfection entirely. The assembly of heaven is still in some fashion "on its way." It forms a single Church with its earthly members, and forms a solidarity with all people of the earth. Nothing is completed without Christ, toward whom everything is created, and without the mother of Jesus, who sums up the history of the sanctification of the Church in her life.

What is the grace that the last day will bring? No one can imagine (cf. 1 Cor 2:9). "…we ourselves, who have the first fruits of the Spirit, groan inwardly while we wait…" (Rom 8:23). God alone knows what the Spirit desires by these groanings (cf. Rom 8:27). Thus theology must be very careful in trying to speak about the last day.

However, we do know this: the grace of the last day is Christ himself revealed and made known. We will "be like him, for we will see him as he is" (1 Jn 3:2).

"As he is," a life-giving spirit. Humanity will be transformed into his image and will also be a spiritual body (cf. 1 Cor 15:44) in power and glory (cf. Phil 3:21).[253] Humanity will live just as does the Holy Spirit, who is the power of love. A spiritual body is totally personalized, totally relational. Not only capable of loving, it exists by loving, and by giving itself.

Corporeal human beings are not fully human as long as they live on earth. The human being is body and possesses a body.

Being body, we are in communication with our bodies. But having a body, we are not entirely relational. To have something is, in fact, antirelational. What you keep you do not give away. Private property is something not given to another. The body is a means of communion, but is opposed to total communion. On earth Jesus loved his disciples, but he lived at their side. In his glorifying death, his human being was fully personalized in the Holy Spirit.[254] His body became entirely relational–capable of itself being given. Jesus now lives in his disciples and they live in him (cf. Jn 14:20). He is given to them in total, as the Eucharist bears witness. Raised as a "spiritual body," each person truly lives by giving him or herself, by "being made capable of love" in Christ who is the universal One, existing before all others. With him, a person is "a life-giving Spirit" and is a source of life for others to the degree of the fullness of his or her own life. The communion of saints will reach its perfection in the final resurrection.

According to Paul's faith, all of creation will share in the grace of the last day. Creation will share in the freedom of the children of God (cf. Rom 8:19). The earthly person and creation each exercise a mutual domination and are, therefore, subject to a mutual slavery. The human person rules over creation, makes use of it and often abuses it. But the human person makes use of it only by submitting him or herself to its laws that lead inescapably to death. Having become a spiritual body, the person will live, like the Risen One, only by the Spirit of God. Then the saying will have its full validity: "For freedom Christ has set us free" (Gal 5:1). Initially head of creation and subject to its laws, a person liberated from all dependence will be all the more creation's head in communion with Christ in whom everything is created. As a spiritual body in total gift of self, each person will be in relationship with material creation more than it was before death. Creation will thus become free as those who live in God's glory (cf. Rom 8:21). A new order will be set up: Jesus'

147

Resurrection reverberates over the people whose head he is, it reverberates over the creatures of which humans are the head. Thus the saying is verified: "All belong to you, and you belong to Christ, and Christ belongs to God" (1 Cor 3:22–23). The bond in this mutual belonging is the Spirit of the resurrection. That Spirit is liberty since love is a bond that liberates.

The Christian can form a certain but only remote concept of the mysterious grace of the final resurrection (cf. 1 Cor 2:9). First, we can imagine what it will be like from what we know of the Risen One to whose communion we have been called (cf. 1 Cor 1:9). Moreover, we can guess what we will become based on the life we are already living. Christ will come that very day. We will see the One who is already visible (cf. Jn 14:9). "We will be like him, because we will see him as he is" (1 Jn 3:2). From earth the faithful follower is transformed by the Lord who will be contemplated with unveiled faces (cf. 2 Cor 3:18). In this life we, who already are children (cf. Gal 4:6), "groan inwardly while we wait for adoption, the redemption of our bodies" (Rom 8:23). The person will become a spiritual body, and henceforth will not be in the flesh; but in the spirit (cf. Rom 8:9). At the final resurrection those belonging to Christ will form a single body in one mutual act of belonging (cf. 1 Cor 15:23). From earth we constitute the body of Christ, bound to one another by the bond of the Holy Spirit.

But everything is in a state of germination. Jesus raised from the dead is an incomprehensible richness and the final resurrection remains mysterious. If one only knew the seed that contains the cedar, who could imagine it in its majesty?

THE LAST JUDGMENT

Before his death Jesus stated: "Now is the judgment of this world" (Jn 12:31). The great and last judgment was pronounced in the

Passover of Jesus. The evangelist knew nothing other than that. According to John, God gave Jesus power both to raise the dead and to judge them. These are really only one power: to raise the dead and judge them in raising them. "Indeed, just as the Father raises the dead and gives them life, so also the Son…The Father judges no one, but has given all judgment to the Son" (Jn 5:21–22). Christ exercises judgment through his resurrecting action. Some are judged simply in the fact of rising to life: "Anyone who hears my word…has eternal life, and does not come under judgment, but has passed from death to life" (Jn 5:24). For others, the Resurrection turns into a condemnation: "All who are in their graves will come out—those who have done good, to the resurrection of life, and those who have done evil, to the resurrection of condemnation" (Jn 5:28–29).

The texts of Scripture do not present the resurrection and the judgment as successive events. The end comes with the resurrection (cf. 1 Cor 15:24). The judgment pronounced by the Passover of Jesus does not unfold like a spectacular trial,[255] but rather, in the power of God who acts in Christ: "Now is the judgment of this world"—a judgment that produces justice and creates God's form of justice. It is executed as it is pronounced.

In this last judgment Christ judges as final savior. His second coming is the mystery of salvation in all the efficacy of his action: "We are expecting a Savior, the Lord Jesus Christ" (Phil 3:20) to rescue us "from the wrath that is coming" (1 Thess 1:10). The belief that "God did not send the Son into the world to condemn the world, but in order that the world might be saved through him" (Jn 3:17) has eternal value. Jesus was established as judge through the power of his resurrection (cf. Acts 10:42); and his resurrection was for the sake of our justification (cf. Rom 4:25). God saves us in his risen Son by exercising his kind of justice. And he exercises it by leading people to their eternal life.

Since God is Father, his justice is exercised as a father. It works in begetting creation and in giving life. If a person refused God's paternity, the power of the resurrection would condemn that person, even though it was saving them. Such a person would rise in the absurdity of a life that represses life, and an existence that refuses to exist. But will there be some whose refusal to be loved and to love will be greater than the infinite love that wills their salvation?

THE LIFE OF THE WORLD TO COME

"Then we will see face to face" (1 Cor 13:12)—that's what eternal life will be like. What will we see? Thomas Aquinas described the blissful life this way: "The ultimate beatitude can only be in the vision of the divine essence. Perfect beatitude demands that the understanding reach as far as the very essence of the first cause."[256] This definition of the heavenly beatitude dates from a period when a juridical theology of the redemption held sway. Redemption was not understood as a Trinitarian mystery regarding Christ in his filial status. But, like redemption, heaven is a mystery that is both linked to Christ and is Trinitarian.

God begets the Son. The Son is the Father's heaven in the world so that he may also be humanity's heaven (cf. Eph 2:6). It is said that heaven is not a place, but a state of happiness. However, in some way it is a place, a place that is personal. Jesus had made it clear that he himself is the kingdom of God (cf. Lk 11:20, 17:21).[257] The faithful follower lives on this earth in that place. In dying, the faithful follower does not move, to another spot. While on earth our Christian citizenship is already heavenly; having become totally heavenly after death, it will be fully Christian.

To be sure, "Then comes the end when he [Christ] hands over the kingdom to God the Father" (1 Cor 15:24). But he will not abdicate in order to reenter the ranks,[258] because it is "the eternal kingdom of our Lord and savior Jesus Christ" (2 Pet 1:11), who is "the same yesterday and today and forever" (Heb 13:8). To be saved is to be with Christ and like the One who is salvation. "We will be with the Lord forever" (1 Thess 4:17).

In his ardent desire to be with Christ (cf. Phil 1:23) Saint Paul did not merely long to live in God's company. Even here on earth he had clothed himself with Christ (cf. Gal 3:27) and lived in Christ; he hoped to know him in a communion that is even more intimate (cf. Phil 3:10–14). That intimacy is promised by the sacrament that anticipates the eternal banquet: "Those who eat my flesh and drink my blood abide in me and I in them" (Jn 6:56). Salvation resides in this intimate communion, for Jesus Christ is the heavenly space in person.

Linked to Christ, heaven is Trinitarian. To live in intimate communion with the Son whom the Father begets is to live entirely from God's paternity and to experience the Son whom the Father begets by loving him in the Holy Spirit. His family will know God by being co-born with him, that is, by being begotten by the Father with him (cf. Rom 8:29). Such knowledge of God is not simply grasping a fact, it is the very essence of eternal life. Jesus is its mediator. On earth the Scripture quote "No one knows the Father except the Son and anyone to whom the Son chooses to reveal him" (Mt 11:27) was already valid.

However, Christ's vision which he mediates is firsthand: "Then we will see face to face" (1 Cor 13:12) without an intermediary. The reason they will see is because they have been incorporated into the birth of the Son. "Heirs of God and joint heirs with Christ" (Rom 8:17), they will share his filial knowledge. The Father will open their eyes by begetting them in his Son.

Such a knowledge is incomprehensible (cf. 1 Cor 13:12). Hence, it is similar to the way God knows. God's being is basically one of knowing, and God knows each person in his creation of them.

In turn, all children of God will know their Father through his act of begetting-creating them.

All this will come to pass in the Holy Spirit: "He will guide you to all truth" (Jn 16:13) in perfect knowledge, for he is the power by which the Father begets the Son by loving him. God's love seals the communion of the Son with his sisters and brothers. The "joy" of the Holy Spirit is found throughout Scripture.[259] Great must be the happiness of Christ and of those who belong to him to be unceasingly born of their Father in the infinity of his love for them.

Here on earth the Church is already an assembly "in God the Father and the Lord Jesus Christ" (1 Thess 1:1), and in "communion of the Holy Spirit" (2 Cor 13:13). Our regular gathering as Church will be fulfilled at last by the grace of the final resurrection. The Spirit, who, as God is one person in two others, also unifies Christ and humanity into a single body through one birth. That is how the plan of God is carried out—the God who creates by speaking in the plural: "Let us make humankind in our image" (Gen 1:26). God wills that humanity be like him: many and one.

Chapter Eleven

THE HOLY SPIRIT AS A MIRROR OF THE PASCHAL MYSTERY

A t the end of this study it seems appropriate to look once again at the role played by the Holy Spirit. A theology of the redemption that ignores the Holy Spirit's role—generally, the juridical theologies—are seriously deficient. All the preceding pages would also be deficient to the extent that they did not express sufficiently the universal presence of the Spirit. For "the spirit of the Lord has filled the world" (Wis 1:7). It is fitting that our final chapter should attempt to replenish that insufficiency.

To enumerate all over again the effects of action by the Spirit would be tedious. Its action deserves to be studied in itself, such as it manifests itself in the Passover of Jesus. To study this action is to study the Spirit in its very mystery. And the Spirit's mystery is to serve as the action of God who begets his Son by loving him.

THE HOLY SPIRIT, ACTION OF GOD

God raised Jesus in the Holy Spirit. Paul said so in Romans 1:4 and repeated it when he announced that God will raise the faithful with Christ in the Holy Spirit.²⁶⁰ Paul confirmed it when he stated that the resurrection of Jesus and the faithful is the work of the power and the glory,²⁶¹ since the Spirit is that power and that glory.

In his various manifestations, the Spirit reveals himself as divine action. He is neither the author nor the effect of the action—he *is* the action itself. The Father raised Jesus; Jesus is raised, and the Spirit is the power of that resurrection. The Spirit is neither the glorifier nor the one glorified. Rather, the Spirit is the glory of the Father who glorifies Jesus. The Father enabled Jesus to die obediently, but the dying of Jesus toward his Father was the Holy Spirit: "Through the eternal Spirit [he] offered himself" (Heb 9:14). The Father gave the anointing; the Son received it; and the Spirit is the anointing.²⁶² The Father is the truth; the Son is its reflection (cf. Heb 1:3), the Spirit guides us to the truth (cf. Jn 16:13). The Spirit is not the one who prays, nor the one who hears the prayer—the Spirit is the cry of the prayer (cf. Gal 4:6). The Spirit is not, like the Father and the Son, the one to whom we give our faith. Rather, the Spirit is the one who enables us to believe²⁶³ and to profess our faith (cf. 1 Cor 12:3).

The paschal mystery brings this primary and definitive light on the mystery of the Spirit: the Spirit is the working power and the divine dynamism of the Godhead. Saint Cyril of Alexandria said, "He effects all the works of God."²⁶⁴

The most powerful of these works is the resurrection that raised Jesus up to God's lordship. God's action of raising is paternal. Jesus was begotten into filial fullness. While raising him, God made this pronouncement: "Today I have begotten you" (Acts 13:33). Must we not conclude from this that the Spirit is the power in which the Father begot Christ? The infancy narratives already attest to it: Jesus is the Son conceived by God in the Holy Spirit. Under the action of the Spirit he received his identity as Man/Son of God (cf. Lk 1:35). The Spirit of God is the Father's spirit in his paternity, and is the Son's spirit (cf. Gal 4:6) in his loving obedient relationship with the Father. The Spirit's mystery lies in God's act of begetting.

Scripture offers a precise description of the Spirit's power. The Holy Spirit is love: "Hope does not disappoint us, because God's love has been poured into our hearts through the Holy Spirit that has been given to us" (Rom 5:5). The relationship between the Spirit and the love of God is affirmed implicitly and yet with sharpness. The love of God is poured out by the gift of the Spirit. The Spirit is "poured out"—that verb is a common characteristic of the gift of the Spirit.[265] The gift is the pledge of final salvation according to Romans 8:23.[266] There it is the presence of God's love that offers the guarantee. The charity of the faithful follower is a fruit of the presence of the Spirit in him or her (cf. Gal 5:22). The phrases "in the Spirit" and "in charity" hardly differ in meaning.[267] The flesh and the Spirit contradict each other like egoism and love. Charity can be called "the charity of the Spirit." The only time the Spirit is cited by the author of Colossians is in this phrase: "Your love in the Spirit" (cf. Col 1:8). And Saint Paul called to mind a communion of the Holy Spirit (cf. 2 Cor 13:13).[268] The Spirit is the bond that makes many into a single body: "In the one Spirit we were all baptized into one body" (1 Cor 12:13).[269] Love is the bond that unites two beings, for example, a husband and wife into a single body. We can then conclude from this that charity is a characteristic mark of the Holy Spirit.[270]

If, therefore, the Spirit is the power in which God raised Jesus —that is to say, the Spirit is God's infinite power of love—then God raised Jesus by loving him. If the Resurrection is a begetting, God begets by loving. Begotten in this way, Jesus is the Father's "Son, the beloved" (Mt 3:17).

It is of capital importance for any theology of the Holy Spirit to know that the Spirit is the action of the Father who begets and of the Son who hands himself over and lets himself be begotten. Descriptions like "to beget," "the power of begetting," and "to be father" as applied to God are only images, but they evoke a divine reality.

THE HOLY SPIRIT, THE DEPTH OF GOD

Theology distinguishes between each divine person and the divine nature shared by the Trinity. It lists the multiple attributes of God's nature: omnipotence, holiness, indivisible unity, irrepressible life, love, and so on. Scripture uses the term "divine nature" only in a later writing (cf. 2 Pet 1:4).[271] But it says a great deal about the Spirit of God in ways that differ very little from what we understand by "divine nature." The study of the paschal mystery allows us to believe that those divine attributes common to the Father and the Son are also proper to the Spirit.

Omnipotence is the first attribute and it gives its name to God: "The Mighty One has done great things for me" (Lk 1:49). It unfolds its infinite breadth in the Resurrection (cf. Eph 1:19–22), conferring on Jesus "power that also enables him also to make all things subject to himself" (Phil 3:21). The power that makes Jesus "Lord" equally with God (cf. Phil 2:9–11) is another name for the Holy Spirit: "You will receive power when the Holy Spirit has come upon you" (Acts 1:8). Jesus lives by the power of that Spirit who raised him (cf. Rom 8:11; 2 Cor 13:4). He had been conceived by the Spirit and the power (cf. Lk 1:35).

The power of the Resurrection is an absolute paradox; it does not suppress the death of Jesus,[272] yet it is released there. It shows itself impressively in the weakness of the cross (cf. 1 Cor 1:17–25). The affinity of the Spirit of power with death is remarkable.

God is holy. Holiness is the biblical word for transcendence.

The Spirit is the expression of that transcendence. The Spirit is the reality of God from on high. Saint Basil says, "Its proper and peculiar title is Holy Spirit."[273] Raised in the Spirit, Jesus was fully sanctified, that is to say, he was totally "divinized" (cf. Jn 17:19).[274] Before him Thomas prostrated himself: "My Lord and my God!" (Jn 20:28). Jesus truly became the Holy One, as announced before his birth: "The Holy Spirit will come upon you [Mary]...therefore the child to be born will be holy" (Lk 1:35). The mystery of God's holiness belongs in a special way to the Holy Spirit.

The holiness revealed in the Resurrection of Jesus is also a paradox. In the Old Testament holiness calls to mind a notion of separation.[275] But in the Passover of Jesus, holiness was communicated as something inherent in humanity. The divine character of holiness totally overflows in Jesus as life-giving spirit who became the universal One, existing before all else. Yet he exists in solidarity with sinful humanity through his holiness.[276]

To be spirit is another attribute of divinity: "God is spirit, and those who worship him must worship in Spirit and truth" (Jn 4:24). It is not the immateriality of God that is addressed in prayer and worship, but his vibrant fullness of being. This is distinct from earthly realities which are transient, for example, the cult celebrated in Jerusalem or on the mountain of Samaria which are incapable of sanctifying. When Paul spoke of a living spirit, he obviously did not mean an immaterial being. When he contrasted the spirit and the letter, he was distinguishing between the depth of reality which cannot be understood and what we can observe on the surface (cf. 2 Cor 3:4–18). God is Spirit. He is the real One in supreme fullness. "Spirituality" refers to divine holiness and its transcendence. The Holy Spirit is both holy and spirit. The Spirit is the personal expression of the divine attribute we call "spirituality."

The paradox is blatant. God's fullness of being overflowed

and transformed the man Jesus at his death when he was no longer anything in himself. His material human body contained the presence of the Holy Spirit. From there the Holy Spirit sprang forth into the world. "'Out of the believer's heart shall flow rivers of living water.' Now he said this about the Spirit" (Jn 7:38–39). Sprung forth from the body of Christ, the Spirit gathers the faithful in this body (cf. 1 Cor 12:13). An unusual affinity exists between pure divine spirituality and material creation with its limits.

God is the Living One. That is another of his attributes. He never stops proclaiming in Scripture: "I live." The Holy Spirit is that irrepressible life (cf. Rom 8:2). Jesus was "put to death in the flesh, but made alive in the spirit" (1 Pet 3:18); he "was crucified in weakness, but lives by the power of God" (2 Cor 13:4). Having become a life-giving spirit, Jesus is the universal resurrection from the dead (cf. Rom 1:4) [NAB].[277] Even there the Holy Spirit is *in person* one of the attributes of divinity.

The Resurrection of Jesus in the Holy Spirit is life in death. There more than anywhere else the paradox is striking. In John 19:30 the gift of the Spirit, God's breath, is symbolized by the last breath of Jesus on the cross. Water, another symbol of the Spirit (cf. Jn 7:37–39), flows from Christ's pierced side. The resurrection in the power of the Spirit constitutes a unique mystery with Jesus. In death Jesus was born as Son of God. There again is that strange affinity of the Spirit with death![278]

In the Resurrection, Jesus was vindicated (cf. 1 Tim 3:16). Because of the Resurrection in the Holy Spirit, Jesus was inundated by holiness, and by God's justice. Holiness and divine justice are similar concepts: Jesus addressed God as "Holy Father" and "righteous" (cf. Jn 17:11, 25), Jesus became righteousness and sanctification by rising in the Holy Spirit (cf. 1 Cor 1:30). The divine attribute of justice is granted especially to the Spirit.

Contrary to human justice, the Spirit's justice is not exercised by punishing deviates and rewarding the just. Rather, it justifies anyone who receives it when it communicates itself. It is a justice of the resurrection that is loving and creative.

God is one. Unity is an essential attribute of God. Faith in the divinity of Jesus was never intended to contradict the unity of God. On earth Jesus lived with a certain type of estrangement from the Father. Yet when he rose in the Holy Spirit, the expression: "The Father and I are one" (Jn 10:30) was fully verified. The Spirit is the bond of their communion. The Spirit is the love of Father for the Son, and vice versa. Theology likes to say: God is one in the unity of the divine nature. But the liturgy is closer to what Scripture actually says. Liturgy speaks of the unity of the Father and the Son *in* the Holy Spirit.[279]

There, too, the paradox is glaring because the unity of the Trinity is realized amid extreme diversification. In the Father, the Spirit is the infinite power of generation; in Christ, the Spirit is infinitely open to death. Thus the Spirit unifies despite the pull of those opposite actions. God is one, but not in the sense of single unit. That is a poor example of unity because we can add to it an unlimited quantity single units. But God is one and cannot be added to. God is a tri-unity in the Spirit who brings about infinite diversity with absolute unity.[280]

"God is love," and sending the Son into the world proves that (cf. 1 Jn 4:8–9). The Holy Spirit is love. Everything that characterizes God is personified in the Spirit. Different from God's other attributes, love does not contain any paradox or anything else that appears contrary to authentic human love. The same words can be used to express both the love of God and human love. Those paradoxes mentioned above are explained by love. Because the all-powerful One is love, it is sacrificed in a confusing humility and never imposes divine rule. Since God is love, holiness does not separate anything from him, not even the person who is farthest away through sin. Love, as the most interior quality causes anyone who loves to give totally of themselves. Love is infinite. It desires to go infinite distances. The relationship of the Spirit to death is not surprising if we realize that deep love nourishes in itself the desire both to die and to live. In his death Jesus performed his highest loving act. If justice is identified with love, it is exercised only in loving, pardoning, and communicating itself. Justice is swallowed up in the force of the Resurrection of Jesus, who is in solidarity with sinners. As was said above, as love, the Holy Spirit diversifies as much as it unites. Thus, those who love one another become more truly themselves by entering into communion with others. All the paradoxes are resolved in the Spirit of love. In that Spirit two infinitely opposite beings, named the Father and the Son, meet and constitute only one. In the paschal mystery where all these paradoxes meet again, they are ruled by one law that unifies them: "...so that the world may know that I love the Father" (Jn 14:31).

If it is true that the divine attributes are made explicit in the Spirit, there is no place to identify that Spirit with the divine nature the way theology understands it, since by definition divine nature is impersonal. But already in the Hebrew Scriptures the Spirit characterizes everything that is contained in the word "God."[281] In the New Testament, the Holy Spirit is on high, God is "spiritual," and God's characteristics are manifested in the Spirit. Augustine of Hippo favorably recorded the opinion of several thinkers of his time: "Some, however, have gone so far as to believe that the communion of the Father and the Son, and (so to speak) their Godhead *(deitatem)*, which the Greeks designate *theotēs,* is the Holy Spirit;...This Godhead, then, which they wish to be understood likewise as the love and charity subsisting between these two [Persons], the one toward the other, they affirm to have received the name of the Holy Spirit."[282] Reflecting on the paschal mystery leads us to think that the Holy Spirit is in person what is described about the divine nature. Does that not mean that God is essentially Father who begets a Son, so that the nature of God is Trinitarian? For the Spirit is the power in which God raised Jesus, and in which he begot the Son. Meister Eckhart has said: "The highest aspiration of God is to beget."[283] He is equally Father and God in begetting the Son. God is infinite paternity in the Spirit with relation to the Son. God's paternity includes everything: in the Holy Spirit God begets the Son and enables him to let himself be begotten in the Spirit. It is not surprising that Scripture reserves the name of God for the Father: "There is one God, the Father...and one Lord, Jesus Christ" (1 Cor 8:6).

THE SPIRIT OF JESUS, SON OF GOD

Not everything is included about Jesus when we call him the Man/God. Not everything is included about the Holy Spirit when we speak about the divine attributes personified in it. The full identity of Jesus is Man/Son of God. That is how he is revealed in the paschal mystery; that is how he is Man/God, the Holy One of God. The Holy Spirit, in its profound truth, reveals itself in the same mystery as the Son. It is the Spirit of the Father in his paternity and of Jesus in his relationship to the Father. Its identity is as Spirit of God who is both Father and Son.

The Spirit is active; the divine attributes personified in it are dynamic. The Spirit is present in Jesus as the power of filialization, life-giving, spiritualizing, and as love that gives birth. Through the Spirit, Jesus attained the full truth of who he was from his origin: Man/Son of God. The Spirit is involved in the filial mystery of Jesus. To the name "Spirit of God" in the Hebrew Scriptures, are added "Spirit of his Son" (Gal 4:6), "Spirit of Jesus" (Phil 1:19), "Spirit of Christ" (Rom 8:9), and "Spirit of the Lord" (2 Cor 3:17). Thus the identity of the Spirit becomes more precise: it is the Spirit of God and of Jesus in their relationship as Father and Son.

There is only one Holy Spirit, but it varies in function depending on whether it is in God or in Christ. In one, it is Spirit of the Father; in the other, it is Spirit of the Son. It is Spirit of God in his paternity and Spirit of Christ in his relationship to the Father. In this way the paschal mystery reveals the Spirit as both the power of the Father who raised Jesus and begot him to full sonship, and as an offering of oneself to God in Christ (cf. Heb 9:14). The Spirit that we possess in our communion with Christ is called the "spirit of adoption" in which we cry "Abba!" (cf. Rom 8:9, 15).[284] Jesus also prayed in that way (cf. Mk 14:36). The Spirit belongs to Jesus in his relationship as Son and to the Father in his paternity.

Acting different in God and in Christ, the Spirit is also possessed by each of them differently. Jesus possesses the Spirit obediently by receiving it. Certainly Jesus possesses the Spirit infinitely, but he was given that Spirit "without measure" (Jn 3:34). If, in being glorified, Jesus became the source of the Holy Spirit for us, then that source is nourished by the Father (cf. Jn 7:37–39).

The Father and Christ both possess the Spirit; the Spirit is their fullness which they give away. The Father and the Son act through the Spirit. But the Holy Spirit is not like them. The Spirit has no fullness, and nothing comes from it. Rather, the Spirit belongs to the Father and the Son, and is entirely at their service. The Spirit cultivates a unique connection with Jesus who in his death had nothing, was nothing, and became completely "for others." The Holy Spirit is divine humility.[285]

THE SPIRIT AS IT EXISTS IN THE TRINITY

Can we ascertain the Spirit's role in the eternal Trinity based on the role it plays in Christ? Some theologians deny that this is possible. They dissociate the role the Spirit plays in the economy of salvation from its role in Trinitarian theology, believing that knowing one would not allow us to understand the other. But those theologians do not take into account, as far as I know, the Passover of Jesus and its mystagogical role.[286]

Jesus knew God[287]—who can deny that? On earth Jesus revealed God to us: "No one knows the Father except the Son and anyone to whom the Son chooses to reveal him" (Mt 11:27). Jesus is "the image of the invisible God" (Col 1:15), "the exact imprint of God's very being" (Heb 1:3). This God, whom "no one has ever seen," has been made known to us by Jesus (cf. Jn 1:18). "I have made known to you everything that I have heard from my Father" (Jn 15:15). Without Jesus we would not know about the mystery of the Trinity; and we would know about the Spirit only what Scripture of the First Testament offers.

Jesus is the one who left the Father (cf. Jn 13:3). His coming into the world delayed his eternal coming. There was no break in continuity between the Word in its eternity and the Word in his humanity. If there had been, would he still be the Word Incarnate? In being glorified with the Father (cf. Jn 17:5), Jesus was seated at the Father's right hand (cf. Mt 26:64), fully divine as the eternal Word. His name is the "Word of God" (Rev 19:13). In the mystery of his death and glorification, God reveals Jesus' identity as eternal Son, born of God in the Holy Spirit. The Spirit is the mediator of communion in the Trinitarian mystery, and we live by knowing that mystery: "This is eternal life, that they may know you" (Jn 17:3). We are co-born with Christ and in him we know God. In his Passover, Jesus is the entrance for others into the Trinitarian mystery. Theology tries to describe what the faithful know through their life in communion with Christ. Although only a pale reflection of the real reality, the concepts theology proposes are true.[288] It is certain that the paschal mystery allows us to acquire a vision of the eternal Trinity.

The paschal mystery shows us two dimensions of God: the Father who raised Jesus and begot him, and the Son who, in his death, let himself be begotten. That mystery is carried out by the Holy Spirit. Hence we can also think of the Trinity as having two dimensions with the relationship of paternity and filiation being carried out by the Holy Spirit. This concept means that the Spirit is not something added to the Father's infinite outreach toward the Son. The same love emanates from God in the relationship of the Father to the Son in the Trinity as it does in the two-dimensional mystery of Christ's Passover.[289] The love that emanates from the Father does not go beyond the Son, nor does it branch off in another direction toward a third person outside the relationship of the Father and the Son. Since God is essentially Father, his action is unique and it is consumed in begetting his Only Son. The third Person of the Trinity does not exist apart from the Father's unique action, nor after God has finished acting. The third Person is itself that action of God. That is how the third Person is present in the paschal mystery where the Father gives fullness of life to the Son who willingly receives that life by dying. The Spirit is the life-giving power. The Spirit does not constitute a third dimension. It does not come after the Father and the Son. It is not added to them. Rather, everything they do is accomplished by the Spirit.

The Spirit ordinarily occupies the third place in the Trinity. That is appropriate for the one who personifies the humility of God. Often Scripture does not even mention the Spirit with the other two Persons. But the third Person is not really last. The third Person does not follow the others either in time or even in logic—the third Person is simultaneous with them.

Without being the beginning, the Spirit was present at the beginning; without being the completion, it is present at the completion. If the Father begets, it is always through the Spirit. If the Son lets himself be begotten, it is always through the Spirit. The Father and Son are two in the Spirit, and are inconceivable without the Spirit in the Father's paternity or in the Son's lovingly obedient relationship. The same is true in the paschal mystery: the Father did not raise Jesus without the life-giving power of the Spirit, and the Son was not raised without "the eternal spirit" in whom he was offered (cf. Heb 9:14). The Spirit is in the middle. The Spirit *is* the middle. The paschal mystery was carried out by the Spirit. Again, the same must be true for the Trinity.

The Spirit is love; in God everything is carried out by loving (cf. 1 Jn 4:8). The Trinity is three: the Begetter, the Begotten, and the divine Power of Begetting. Augustine said, "They are three: the Lover, the Loved One, and Love."[290] The Lover begets the Loved One by loving. The Spirit is the middle Person[291] common to the two others. The mystery is carried out in the fire that sets the Father and the Son ablaze.

Although the Spirit is common to them both, the Father and the Son are infinitely different amid their indivisible unity. The paschal mystery illustrates how the Father and the Son meet in their infinite differences: in the unlimited power of life and freedom from death; in the fullness of the Father's giving and of Christ's receiving. The Spirit is the one in whom the Father gives himself, and in whom the Son receives the Father.

The Spirit is able to infinitely diversify itself so that it can be the Spirit of the Father in giving, and, at the same time, the Spirit of the Son in receiving. In loving, one gives oneself to another while receiving the other for oneself. Love has the two aspects of giving and receiving. In the Spirit, the Father gives himself and, in giving, receives the Son; the Son receives the Father and, receiving, gives himself to the Father. Love is both gift and reception. But first it is gift in the Father and reception in the Son. Only thereafter does it become reception by the Father and the giving of self by the Son.

Theologians ordinarily do not present the Trinitarian mystery as a two-dimensional scheme in which all emanation proceeds entirely from the Father to the Son through the power of the Holy Spirit. According to some, the Father begets the Son and, then "breathes forth" the Spirit.[292] According to others, the "breathing forth" of the Spirit is done through the Son, even though the Son has no active part in "breathing forth" the Spirit. According to the most widespread theory in Latin theology, the Father and the Son "breathe forth" the Holy Spirit not as Father and Son but in their unity as God. One can formulate various criticisms of these theories. Let it suffice to say that they seem to ignore the fact that in Scripture the Spirit is the Power-Person of God. Moreover, they do not ask about the paschal mystery from which faith in the Trinity arose. In those systems the third Person is last, and it only comes afterward—as an outcome of the Trinity's activity. From the Father proceeds the Son; from the Father and the Son proceeds the Holy Spirit, according to Catholic thought. But nothing proceeds from the Holy Spirit. Hence some have been able to speak of a "holy sterility" of the Holy Spirit.[293]

But there is nothing like that in the paschal mystery. The third Person is not last there. The Holy Spirit did not spring forth in Christ after the Resurrection. At the beginning of his earthly life, the Spirit did not come to Jesus after his conception. Jesus was conceived and was raised in the Holy Spirit. The Spirit is not unproductive in Christ nor in his faithful ones. It is in the Spirit that Christ and the faithful are born.

In the same way, in the Trinity (it must be repeated) the Spirit does not come in last, and did not spring forth after the Son was begotten. The Spirit is not the completion of the Trinitarian activity. No, the Spirit is itself the activity, the power to beget, and the force of love through which the Father begets. Far from being unproductive, the Spirit is divine generativity.

The total being of the Father exists in his paternity, infinitely begetting. It is, therefore, from God's paternity that the Spirit proceeds. However, the Spirit is not a "second son" because the paternity of God is totally consumed in begetting the Only Son. The Trinitarian mystery has only two dimensions. Although the Spirit proceeds from the Father's paternity, the Spirit is not a son. Rather, the Spirit is the power of the process of begetting. The mystery of paternity and of sonship is carried out in the Spirit.[294]

It would be surprising if, in creating the world, the Trinitarian God did not put his stamp on his work. But he has: "God created humankind in his image / ...male and female he created them. / God blessed them, and God said, 'Be fruitful'" (Gen 1:27–28). Christian intuition perceives a Trinitarian reflection in the human family where a father begets a child in a maternal womb and begets it by loving. This law that rules nature also governs the life of all children of God: they are "born of water and the Spirit" (Jn 3:5).[295] Water is a feminine and maternal symbol as well as a symbol of the Holy Spirit.[296]

From among all women who are mothers, there is one who is blessed. She has not only played a role like that of the Spirit, she has played it in synergy with the Spirit during the birth of God's Son into the world: "The Holy Spirit will come upon you, and the power of the Most High will overshadow you; therefore the child to be born will be called holy; he will be called Son of God" (Lk 1:35). God begot the Son into this world through the Holy Spirit and in the womb of a woman. The unique mystery of begetting is played out on two levels: one heavenly, the other earthly. Mary is the human understudy of the Holy Spirit. Jesus was born Son of God as well as "of the Spirit" and "of Mary" (cf. Mt 1:16).[297]

The paschal mystery was already announced. And although the Spirit worked in conjunction with a woman in Jesus' earthly birth, it worked alone in Christ's birth to filial fullness. No creature could participate in that. In that work, especially, the Spirit appears like a womb in which the Son of God was born. Jesus rose as Son of God (cf. Acts 13:33) in the Holy Spirit (cf. Rom 8:11).

Today theologians no longer hesitate to speak of the maternal role of the Holy Spirit. A modern saint has written: "Who is the Father? What is his personal life? To beget—for he begets the Son eternally....The Father begets, the Son is begotten, and the Spirit is the power of conception. And that describes their personal life by which they are distinguished among themselves. ...The Spirit is, therefore, this very holy, infinitely holy, immaculate conception."[298] Mary in her motherhood is its reflection.

Two of the Persons in the Trinity have names: Father and Son. The third Person is the most mysterious and is called "Breath," something that is not a name. Yet from that third Person, who is God's act of love, God begot his Son into the world, creating the image of a son in the humble handmaid.

The theology of the Holy Spirit presented above can give rise to a lot of critical questions. Can the Spirit be a "person" if it is an action, that is, the power of begetting? Or if it is internal to the other two Persons? A person has a face, an action does not have any. The Spirit is situated vis-à-vis other persons, and is not internal to them. But in Scripture, the Spirit does not have a name or a face and presents itself as internal to the Father and the Son. Theology must yield and admit that in God there is a Person who is pure mystery for some reason. If the Spirit lacks a face, nevertheless it is through the Spirit (through its activity) that the features on the face of the Father and the Son take shape.

Theology wishes that the Trinitarian order of Father, Son, and Holy Spirit be respected. But that order is not a succession. In theological imagery by which God is revealed, the Spirit is the Person who is both third and middle. Thus at the baptism of Jesus where the relationship between God and Jesus appeared, the Holy Spirit was the third element in the scene, but it hovered between the Father and Jesus, his Son. Art has held onto this image to represent the Trinity. It has recaptured it in a more explicitly paschal form where the Father supports on his knees the immolated body of Christ and where the Spirit hovers between the faces of the Father and the Son.

Christians have devised a rich and simple symbol: the sign of the cross. Traced on people, it is a synthesis of the mystery of the Trinity and of redemption. The hand moves from the Father to the Son in a vertical line, signifying that the Trinitarian mystery, like redemption, has two dimensions. The hand then passes across that line, signifying that everything in the Trinity and in redemption is carried out through the Holy Spirit. Named third, the Spirit is at the heart of the paschal mystery and the Trinity; it is the third Person who is present everywhere and always acting. The liturgical doxology glorifies "the Father and the Son in the Holy Spirit."

THE SPIRIT IS THE OUTPOURING OF THE FATHER AND THE SON

If the Spirit is the power of begetting, we could believe that the Son has no part in its outpouring. Yet Scripture speaks of the "Spirit of his Son" (cf. Gal 4:6). Scripture attests that the Spirit is involved in the mystery of the Son, and inseparable from it. Since outpouring is an action, how could the Spirit avoid overflowing into the mystery of the Son? The Holy Spirit is the Spirit of Jesus as much as the breath of Jesus is his breath: "He breathed on them and said to them, 'Receive the Holy Spirit'" (Jn 20:22). That divine person cannot be the Holy Spirit of Jesus unless it is assumed into the eternal Son and is poured out on that eternal son. In his glorification, Jesus is caught in the full mysteriousness of his relationship to the Father. Jesus is eternally being begotten by the Father. Thus we can say the same things about the Christ of glory as we say about the Word that is manifested in him, and vice versa.

The paschal mystery teaches us that Christ shares in the outpouring of the Spirit and that his role is different from that of the Father. Resurrection in the power of the Spirit is the work of the Father. But Jesus also shares in that power: "I lay down my life in order to take it up again....I have power to lay it down, and I have power to take it up again" (Jn 10:17–18). The resurrection in the power of the Spirit, therefore, is also Christ's work: "Destroy this temple, and in three days I will raise it up. He was speaking of the temple of his body" (Jn 2:19–21). Christ shared in the act of his resurrection and therefore he shared in the outpouring of the Spirit on him. Jesus' part was to give consent to the action of the Father in his death. Jesus opened himself to the Father who begot him and who raised him by the power of the Spirit. Jesus' role was to obediently receive from the Father.

The concept of receptive causality, although little used in theology, is of major importance here. It is impossible to make a gift if no one accepts it. A man cannot marry a woman if she does not consent to it. Anyone who accepts a gift empowers someone else to be able to give; the woman who allows herself to be married enables a man to become her husband. Jesus was asked to consent to his eternal begetting. In biblical language, instead of "to consent" one says "to obey." Jesus "became obedient to the point of death–even death on a cross. Therefore God also highly exalted him" (Phil 2:8–9). The Father glorifies Jesus, but only in response to Jesus' obedience: "He learned obedi-

ence through what he suffered; and having been made perfect..."
(Heb 5:8–9). Jesus can claim glorification from the Father just
as he can say, "I sanctify myself" (Jn 17:19). Jesus exercised true
causality. His glorification in the Holy Spirit would not have
taken place if he had not received it. Jesus participated obediently by receiving the outpouring of the Holy Spirit.

Since he was permitted to raise himself from Incarnate Son
to eternal mystery, we can believe that the Son plays a similar
role when the Spirit of the Father overflows to him—he receives
it. It is the Father who begets. The Father is the source of the
Spirit. By the Father's Spirit, he empowers the Son to be lovingly obedient and open to receiving the Father's paternity. But
without the Son, God would not be Father. Without the Son,
who freely gives consent, the Father would not beget, and the
power of the Spirit would not pour out. In the Trinity, every
activity is carried out by each of the three Persons according to
its role as Father or as Son or as Holy Spirit.

The Holy Spirit is the act of loving. In the Spirit, the Father
begets by loving; and by loving, the Son lets himself be begotten. In both of them, the Spirit is love. The Holy Spirit is poured
out to each of them, although differently, and the Son is the one
who receives everything. But, even though he receives everything, the Son shares in the outpouring of the Spirit to the Father himself. For by loving, he induces the Father to love: "For
this reason the Father loves me, because I lay down my life..."
(Jn 10:17). In those who love each other the reciprocity of love
is a mutual inducement to love. By loving, the Son shares in the
outpouring of the Spirit of love to the Father. But the Father is
its source, for the Father is where everything begins.

Thus the Son is not inferior to the Father, although he receives everything. By receiving, he enables the Father to be the
one who gives. He is co-eternal and of equally immeasurable
greatness. Neither is the Spirit inferior; he is the third Person,

not the last person. What the Father and the Son are, they are in the Spirit. The Holy Spirit is a person *in* the other two, at both the beginning and the end. Not only are the Father and the Son one, but the ebb and flow that prevails between them is eternal and supremely intense forever.

All of this is said in the poverty of human words—everything could be said otherwise and better. But in light of the paschal mystery, this truth compels itself: the Spirit is poured out in the relationship of the Father and the Son: in the Father's paternity, and in the Son's lovingly obedient receptivity. That conclusion is of capital importance.

At the end of this journey, the reader has a right to a summary of the theology of the paschal mystery. But this mystery brims over into everything—it is the mystery of the God-Trinity, which is at the heart of creation. How can we compress into a few lines what so many pages have not been able to hold? Still, it is useful to emphasize one last time a few of its points.

In the theology of redemption, the point of departure for reflection is not sin needing to be repaired, nor is it Christ's death as a means to satisfy God's offended justice. Christian faith was born in the encounter with the Risen One; likewise, theological reflection takes its point of departure from the Risen One. He who is the Omega is also the Alpha. The Resurrection is the work of the Father who begets-creates the Son into the world for its salvation. The Resurrection is the summit and the symbol of all the Father's activity—that Father who is the origin of everything. Theology can only understand the death of Jesus in the light of his Resurrection.

The Father acts through the Holy Spirit, whose action is infinite love. The Father eternally begets the Son into the world by loving the Son and all humans created in him. Being unlimited, this love is absolutely gratuitous, and it has no other cause outside itself. Independent of any preliminary activity, it is already at work even before any reparation of sin takes place. The Father realizes all reparation of sin in his Son whom he begot and brought through death to filial fullness on behalf of humans.

One cannot approach this theology without taking into account the necessary expiation of sin. It is God who, in the holiness of his love, "expiates" sin in the biblical sense of the term. God does so through the Lamb who, in solidarity with sinful humanity and by his very holiness, "expiates" sin through his glorifying death. The sin of humanity is enormous, but the holiness of the paschal mystery is even more immense. The holiness of the Paschal mystery is at the heart of the world and wraps it in holiness, drawing the world to itself.

Redemption is a mystery of both death and resurrection. It is realized in an ascent toward the Father, who, through his Son, descended toward our human weakness. Like the angels on Jacob's ladder, theological thought must ascend and descend. We should not distinguish between opposing "ascending theologies" and "descending theologies"—all is one in the Holy Spirit. Christ's death and resurrection each find their meaning in relationship to the other. Through the infinite opposites of death and resurrection, Christ's death and resurrection offer unlimited horizons to theological meditation.

Jesus, dead and risen, is the ultimate epiphany of God. The face of God is unveiled. It is the face of a God-Father whose being is an inexhaustible paternity, and whose omnipresence offers the possibility of infinite self-giving. The Holy Spirit shows itself as the action of that unlimited power of love in which the Father begot the Son and the Son let himself be begotten. He is the Spirit of the Father in his paternity and of the Son in his obedience. Theologians must study the Passover of Jesus before all else in order to understand the mystery of the Trinity.

There are theologies for which the Resurrection is secondary or passed over in silence. The basis of their thought is the sin that needed to be repaired. But the glory of the Father on the face of Christ calls those theologies to participate in a Copernican-type revolution. In reality, it is the Sun that is first, and it makes the Earth rotate around it, giving birth on Easter morning in the light that disperses all darkness. One must hope that these juridical theories—that have influenced the second Christian millennium and contributed to belief in a juridical kind of ecclesiology—will not cross over the threshold of the third millennium.

I have said that the mystery brims over everywhere, and that it is impossible to summarize it in a few lines. Yet an adage exists that make it possible for us to bundle everything together: "That which even the immensities cannot contain, allows itself to be held in something smaller. Such is the way of God."[299] Saint John articulated a saying that captures the equivalent: "God is love" (1 Jn 4:16). The infinite is nothing other than love, it is an immolated omnipotence. For knowledge, as well as for holiness of life, love "binds everything together in perfect harmony" (Col 3:14). That is the summary of what has been said.

Thus we recognize that there is a higher knowledge than theological science. "I will show you a still more excellent way," says Saint Paul (1 Cor 12:31), the way of love that is able to know Christ through communion with him. Theology is only one approach, but the Spirit of love "will guide you into all the truth" (Jn 16:13).

Jesus is God's dwelling among humans, he is the incarnate mystery. To know God, it is necessary to dwell in his house. The one who is the house is also its gate: "I am the gate," says Jesus (Jn 10:9). The Holy Spirit is the key. In the Passover of Jesus, the key of love was turned, and the gate opened wide. It invites us to know God by loving.

NOTES

Preface

1. Such was the custom until recently—a custom that is more or less respected now.
2. J. Riviere, *Le Dogme de la rédemption dans la théologie contemporaine* (Albi: 1948), 167.
3. I cite very few recent works. I beg their authors and my own readers to kindly excuse me. My eyes, though they do not prevent me from writing, make reading too painful.

Chapter 1

4. Ordinarily one translates: "He was established Son of God in power by his resurrection from among the dead." It is, to be sure, a question of the Resurrection of Jesus. But the original text says: "by the resurrection of the dead." Here the faith of the early communities finds expression, according to which the Resurrection of Jesus is the eschatological event.
5. Eph 2:5; Col 2:12; 3:1–3.
6. Later creeds will be developed. There will be the Apostles' Creed and then the Nicene Creed.
7. Exegetes are in agreement that this formula is pre-Pauline. "He rose" is a translation of the Aramaic. In the language of Saint Paul, Jesus "is raised."
8. Apart from the phrase "in the power," the language of Romans 1:3–4 is non-Pauline and reverts to the Judeo-Christian communities.
9. Cf. Rom 4:25; 1 Cor 1:23; 2:2; 15:3.
10. Acts 13:33; Rom 1:1–4; 1 Cor 12:3.
11. Christ is a title of glory in the primitive preaching (cf. Acts 2:36). Paul preaches "a Christ crucified," a crucified Lord of glory.
12. Col 1:19; 2:9.
13. Rev 3:14; 21:6; 22:3.
14. Rev 21:6; 22:13.
15. Chapter nine will treat at greater length this primacy of Christ.

Chapter 2

16. Cf. Jn 4:29; 7:40–41.
17. Cf. Mt 21:16; Lk 19:40.
18. Mt 21:5.
19. Mt 26:64; Eph 1:20–21; Heb 1:3–4; cf. 1 Cor 15:25.
20. 2 Cor 13:4; cf. Eph 1:18–22; Col 2:12.
21. Ps 104:30; 33:6. Cf. Gen 1:2; Job 34:14–15.
22. Rev 1:6; 4:11; 5:12–13; 15:8; 19:1.
23. 1 Pet 4:14; cf. 2 Cor 3:18.
24. Note: In the original French, the author here makes a point that the passage quoted from Ephesians 1:19–21, "*la suréminente grandeur de la piussance, la vigueur, la force déployée dans le Christ en sa **résurrection des morts**"* uses terminology identical to Romans 1:4: "***résurrection des morts***." However, official English translations of those two passages are not identical, and so the reference has been omitted in this edition.
25. With regard to this "divinization" see below, p. 31–35.
26. Phil 2:10. God has "bestowed" on Jesus the supreme name. Everything is a gratuitous gift in the mystery of redemption as well as in the glory merited by his merit by Jesus. His merit consists in welcoming the gift of God.
27. In this pre-Pauline formula, that is foreign to the apostle's vocabulary, the addition "in power" conforms to Pauline language. Perhaps it was inserted by Paul to remove the idea of a filial adoption in the Resurrection.
28. The verb in the present (and not: "I have begotten you") conforms to the Hebrew text. It also conforms to the nature of this enthronement psalm: the king is enthroned today, thought to be begotten by God on the day of his enthronement.
29. 2 Sam 7:13–14; Ps 2:7; 89:27.
30. 1 Cor 1:9; 1 Thess 1:10.
31. There is no next day for Jesus after the resurrection, even if it is said that he appeared the morning, then the evening of Easter, the eighth day….The disciples lived in time. Jesus manifested himself to them in their time. It is the eschatological mystery.
32. Cf. chapters four and nine below.
33. In the New Testament, the word *God* always refers to the Father with a few exceptions that do not contradict this rule.
34. Ambrose, *De excessu fratris sui Satyri*, 9, 1. *CCL* 73, 299. Having been totally divinized, Jesus does not cease to be human. The context in Ambrose is clear.
35. Augustine, *Sermo Guelferb.*, XII. Eu. Morin I, 479: "*Totum hoc resurrectioni militabat.*"
36. Exegetes speak of a divine passive that is frequent in Scripture where God is the author of the action.

37. Basil, *On the Holy Spirit* 16, 39. *SC* 17, 180–181.
38. Mt 3:11; Jn 1:33.

Chapter 3

39. To speak of a becoming in Jesus' filial mystery does not mean that Jesus would not have been the Son from his origin and would have become such through adoption. The theology of the paschal mystery does not expose itself to any suspicion of adoptionism. The Fathers speak of this becoming. Cf. e.g., Hilary, *In Ps. 2*, 27–29; *in Ps. 53*, 14. *CSEL* 22, 57–59. 146: "From being the Son of Man, he is reborn Son of God by the glory of the resurrection."
40. Heb 2:10; 5:5, 9; 7:28.
41. To say, as one does sometimes, that Jesus became aware of his filiation and his messiahship only at the moment of his baptism by John the Baptist does not agree with the intention of this gospel account. It deals, not with a state of consciousness, but with a proclamation of Jesus' relationship with the Father and his messiahship.
42. A son can be in ignorance about the one who begot him. God's paternity is biological, it is relational. A personal relationship is a conscious one. God must have revealed himself as the Father of the human Jesus, because Jesus, even in his humanity, was conscious of it.
43. It is shareable on another level (cf. Mt 11:27), just as Jesus' unique relationship with the Father can be communicated on another level.
44. Jn 2:24–25; 4:16–19 10:14; 13:3.
45. Augustine, *In Joh.*, tract. 106, 7. *CCL* 36, 612–613: "Everything that the Father gives to his Son he gives by begetting."
46. *S. Th.* la 2ae, q. 3, a. 8.
47. Cf. Below, p. 151.
48. Cf. below, p. 39.
49. Rom 8:15; Gal 4:6.
50. John Damascene, *De fide orthodoxa* 3, 24. *PG* 94, 1069.
51. Heb 4:14; 8:1–2; 9:11–12; 10:19–29.
52. Cf. Rom 8:32; Gen 22:16.
53. This is what exegetes call the divine passive.
54. Acts 2:36; 3:14–15; 4:16; 15:30.
55. It is not right to say that God permitted this crime, for to permit is still to grant consent. Rather, he simply did not prevent it.
56. Mt 16:21; 17:22; 20:17 & par.; Jn 3:14.
57. 1 Cor 15:50; cf. Heb 2:10.
58. The kenosis of which Philippians 2:6 speaks extends from the entrance of the Son into the world up to his death (2:6–8). But theology can say that it is

energized in its ultimate depth—Christ's death forms a unique mystery with the Resurrection.

59. Heb 9:13–14; 12:24; 1 Pet 2:2; Rev 7:14.

60. Rom 6:3–11; Eph 2:5–6; Col 2:11–13; 3:1–3; cf. 2 Cor 4:10–12.

61. It goes without saying that from its biological aspect Jesus' death belongs to the past. It is from its human, personal aspect that it is not out of date.

62. Humankind can rejoice—each instant Christ merits salvation for them.

63. Cf., for example, Gen 22:4; Josh 2:17; Jon 2:1.

64. Cf. Strack-Billerbeck, *Kommentar zum N.T. aus Talmud und Midrasch,* I, 747.

65. Cf. Mt 27:52; Rom 1:4 and the note above, p. 1, note #4.

66. Cf. Strack-Billerbeck, op. cit., I, 544.

Chapter 4

67. We, therefore, call this theory the theology of substitution.

68. It is thus that one understands in this theory Jesus' descent into hell, contrary to the primitive tradition found in the Apostles' Creed. There this descent is that of Jesus sharing with the dead his victory over death.

69. Cf. J. Moltmann, *Le Dieu crucifié* (translation; Paris: Cerf, 1978); *Trinité et Royaume* de *Dieu,* ibid. (translation; 1984). A similar soteriology is worked out by H. U. von Balthasar whose thought is presented in: *Les grands textes sur le Christ.* Coll. "Jésus et Jésus Christ," 50 (Paris: Desclée, 1991) 25–34. J. Moingt, *L'homme gui vient* de *Dieu* (Paris: Cerf, 1993) 416 evokes "the idea of a substitutive and expiatory death." The theory has seduced even some orthodox theologians. On this point see J. Kockerols, *L'Esprit* à *la croix* (Brussels: Lessins, 1999) 67–84. This theory finds an echo in modern works on spirituality, for example: M. Zundel, *Je parlerai à ton coeur* (ed. Anne Sigier; Quebec: 1990) 172–175: "God made him sin….Our Lord was obliged to feel that he was guilty of all the faults of the world, as if he were Sin-Made-Man…by living our culpability to the dregs." R. Cantalamessa, *Nous prêchons un Christ crucifié* (translation; ed. des Béatitudes: 1996) 95–105: "The Son of God…became sin, personified sin….In his passion Jesus is impiety, all the impiety of the world. That is why the wrath of God was poured out on him." And there are others.

70. Cf. below, pp. 43–46.

71. For the biblical meaning of the word "expiation," cf. below, pp. 48–51.

72. C. Spicq & P. Grelot, article "blood" in *Voc. de Théol. Bib.* (2d ed.; Paris: Cerf, 1970), 1194.

73. Cf. above, pp. 31–34.

74. Romans 3:24 is ordinarily translated this way: "In virtue of the deliverance accomplished in Christ" (Bible de Jérusalem, Traduction Oecuménique de la Bible) suggests that the deliverance is to be sought in a past act. The Greek

text says: "The deliverance [which is] in Christ Jesus." That suggests the salvation realized by the death of Christ is in the person of Christ. It happens that translators let themselves be guided by the theology they profess. That is perhaps the case here. It is certainly the case in 2 Corinthians 5:21 where the Traduction Oecuménique de la Bible accommodates the translation to the theology of substitution (cf. below, p. 58, note #104).

75. Rom 6:3–11; 8:17; Eph 2:5–6; Col 2:11–12; 2 Tim 2:11.

76. Note: A loose translation of the French version of Romans 1:4 reads: "The resurrection of the dead." The author's point is that Jesus has become "the resurrection of [all] the dead." However, official English translations of Romans use the phrases "was declared to be Son of God…by resurrection *from* the dead" [NAB]. Neither of those changes makes sense inthe way the author intended, and so it has been deleted in this edition.

77. 1 Cor 6:20; 7:23; 1 Pet 1:18.

78. It is the same with suffering. When a Christian says that he or she will offer up his or her sufferings for the welfare of others, such a person suffers in Christ and with him (Rom 8:17). He or she "learns submission to God" (cf. Heb 5:8), and in Christ and with him becomes a principle of salvation. Cf. 2 Cor 4:10–12; Col 1:24.

79. The verb in the passive—"you have been redeemed at a great price"—refers to the Father as agent of this action.

80. Cf. A. Schenker, "Substitution du châtiment ou prix de la paix?" in: *La Pâque du Christ, mystère de salut* (Lectio Divina 112; 1982), 75–90.

81. It is possible that the second part does not belong to the primitive logion. Cf. X. Léon-Dufour, *Face à la mort, Jésus et Paul* (Paris: Seuil, 1979), 94–95.

82. Clement of Alexandria, *Protrepticus* X, 110, 2–3, *SC* 178: "He took on flesh in order to play the drama of salvation in humanity. He was its authentic actor."

83. Augustine, *Ench. ad Laur.* 13, 41: "Because things of the flesh are similar to those of sin, Christ is called sin" (2 Cor 5:21).

84. Gal 4:3; Col 2:8, 20.

85. For the meaning of this expiation, cf. above, pp. 48–51.

86. Col 1:15–17; cf. Jn 1:1–3; 1 Cor 8:6. See below, chapter nine.

87. According to the theory of substitution, Jesus is in solidarity with sinful humanity, not on account of his holiness, but on account of the sins that, despite his innocence, he would bear in himself. This solidarity would affect Jesus in his death. Now Jesus is in solidarity, not with sins, but with sinful humanity. He is such forever because in his very being he is in solidarity with humans.

88. Mt 3:17; 17:5.

89. 1 Cor 15:3; Rom 4:25 pass.

90. There has been talk of an "essential fault" in this theology. R. Tremblay,

"L'Homme (Ep 4,13) mesure de l'homme d'aujourd'hui et de demain," *St Mor* 35 (1997) 104, n. 74. Cf. ibid. 26 (1988) 239–241; 27 (1989) 791–793; 30 (1992) 235–236.

91. *Dictionnaire Larousse*: "To expiate: repair a crime or fault by a punishment or penalty." It is in this sense that the juridical type theologies understand expiation. But sin is not repaired in this way: a person can still remain a criminal while undergoing the appropriate punishment.

92. S. Lyonnet, art. "Expiation," *Voc. de théol. bibl.* (2d ed.; Paris: Cerf, 1970), 426.

93. Let us recall that the formula "in Christ" calls to mind the Christ of glory.

94. It is not to be translated: "after having obtained eternal salvation."

95. Mt 27:35, 39, 43 & par.; Ps 22:19, 8, 9.

96. One often speaks of God's silence during the passion of his Son. One often understands it as a stubborn silence before the distress of Jesus. In the same sense one speaks of the "scandal of the cross." The expression is Paul's (1 Cor 1:23). According to Paul, the cross is a scandal for anyone who does not understand its mystery. Theology itself must look at the cross from the vantage point of a believer! If there is silence on God's part, it is that of patient love that does not unleash thunderbolts against the Son's murderers. God's response cannot be heard with human ears. God's work unfolds in depth and is shown to believers by the Resurrection of Jesus. The evangelists point out that during the passion itself God gave signs of his presence with Jesus: an angel, representing God, strengthens Jesus in Gethsemane; God has the royal status of Jesus proclaimed on the cross; nature mourns (Mt 27:45 and par.); the curtain in the temple is torn. Obviously, God was not deaf to Jesus' distress.

97. Cf. above, p. 30–31.

98. The Christian would also learn with joy that his or her death, too, will be a final and better prayer.

99. Rom 8:34; Heb 7:25.

100. One should think of the justice that the father of the Prodigal Son and the owner who sends workers into the vineyard practiced, as well as the protestations that such justice raises.

101. The way of understanding the mediation of Christ, exclusive or inclusive, constitutes a split between Protestant theology and Catholic tradition that is difficult to surmount. Catholic tradition in practice is always inspired by an inclusive mediation despite the juridical theology that long prevailed.

102. It is true that modern theologians who have again taken up the theory of substitution place the mystery of redemption in the Trinity up to a point, but do so at the expense of the traditional image of the Trinity. They introduce a breach between the Father and Christ that, in their view, would be produced on the cross.

103. It is stated that the theologies that pay little attention to Jesus' Resurrection are fragmentary and lack coherence (cf. above, p. xi–xii). Ordinarily they do not take into account the Holy Spirit. The Spirit is the mystery of communion; it is also a principle of coherence for theological thought.

104. See above, pp. 43–48. Without doubt it is under the influence of the theology of substitution that the Traduction Oecuménique de la Bible translates 2 Corinthians 5:21: "He identified him with sin, so that through him we might become the justice of God." This translation is doubly at fault. Paul writes: "He made him sin," which is explained by Romans 8:3: "God sent his Son in the likeness of sinful flesh." If he is "identified with sin," he is like incarnate sin. Paul writes: "In order that we might become in him justice," which is the attribute of a theology of communion where believers have communion with the justice (holiness) of Christ, dead and raised. "In order that by him..." is compatible with the theory of substitution, but it is a faulty translation.

105. The verb used in John 1:29 can mean either "take away" or "carry." The evangelist always uses it in the sense of "taking away." Jesus is the Lamb of God—he is not compared to a goat. He is God's paschal Lamb. The whole Gospel of John is oriented toward the Passover of Jesus without any allusion to the feast of Atonement or to the scapegoat.

106. 1 Pt 2:24 recalls Isaiah 53:15. Matthew 8:17 evokes another text concerning the Servant of Yahweh: "Surely he has borne our infirmities and carried our diseases" (Isa 53:4). That is talking about Jesus who cured illnesses. Would we conclude, therefore, that Jesus cured the sick by becoming sick like them? He took their illnesses upon himself by curing them through his power. In the same way, he took sins upon himself by abolishing them through the holiness of his death.

Chapter 5

107. 1 Thess 1:9–10; cf. Rom 8:23; 13:11; 1 Cor 1:7–9.

108. Eph 4:30; cf. 1:14.

109. Rev 1:10; 1 Cor 1:8.

110. Cf. above, p. 1.

111. Jn 12:31; 16:11.

112. Cf. above, p. 15.

113. For certain, the appearances to the first disciples were unique, since they were church-founding. Once the Church had been founded, Jesus is from then on seen in the sacramentality of the Church.

114. The language of "return" is, therefore, improper. One does better to speak of "coming," or "advent." Moreover, the word "parousia" does not mean a "return." The resurrection is not a return, nor will be the parousia. To say "return" is to suppose that Christ is absent although promised: "I am coming

to you" (Jn 14:18). Further, it would presume that he will return to the place of his departure and nullify the mystery of his death. But he will not come again because he comes to us constantly.

115. Jn 7:39. The evangelist does not claim that the Spirit did not yet exist or was not already acting (cf. Jn 1:32–33), but simply, that it was not given in the way it is given in Christ. That poses a question about the difference between the grace of the first and of the last Testament.

116. Isa 32:15; 44:3; Ezek 36:25–27 pass.

117. Lk 24:49; Acts 1:4.

118. Acts 2:33; Gal 3:14.

119. Cf. above, p. 11.

120. Jn 14:16–17; 15:26–27; 16:7–15.

Chapter 6

121. Mt 26:64; Mk 14:62.

122. The formula "amen, amen" always confirms the preceding phrase: "The Son of Man will be glorified—amen, he will bear much fruit."

123. The Greek preposition expresses a movement toward, one that unites to Christ.

124. Augustine, *In Joh. tract.* 8. *CCL* 36, 84.

125. Rom 6:3–10; Eph 2:5–6; Col 2:11–13; 3:1–3.

126. 2 Cor 4:10–12; Eph 2:5–6.

127. To return to the theory of redemption by substitution, for in such a theory the death of Jesus is a breach with God. Consequently, could the faithful enter into communion with God by sharing the death of Jesus that is a breach?

128. Jn 10:11–18, 27–28; cf. Rev 5:6; 7:17.

129. Rom 1:7; 1 Cor 1:2. It is not to be translated: "called to become holy." The call itself is sanctifying—the faithful are holy through their call.

130. 1 Thess 5:24; cf. Gal 1:6; 5:8.

131. This mysterious reality that is grace must, therefore, be studied in the light of Jesus' Passover. Here a vast field opens itself to theologians for reflection on the nature and action of grace.

132. Cf. M. A. Chevallier, *Souffle de Dieu* (Paris: Beauchesne, 1991) III, 61–71.

133. Gal 4:4–6; Rom 8:15. It is common to speak of "adoption." Galatians 4:5 is often translated: "God sent his Son that we might receive adoption" (Traduction Oecuménique de la Bible). The term used by Saint Paul (*hyiothesia*) means "adoption" in profane Greek. But Paul understands it in its etymological sense: an act that makes a son, filiation. He is not thinking of adoption: "God sends his Son...so that we may receive filiation, and truly you are sons. To be sure, the lovingly obedient relationship of the faithful differs from that of Christ. John expressed that difference in his vocabulary: Jesus

is "the Son," the faithful are "the children." However, the relationship is real in everyone: "I am ascending to my Father and your Father" (Jn 20:17). Paul uses both terms: "son" and "child." The faithful are not sons by adoption but by participation in the One who is "the elder among many brothers" (Rom 8:29).

134. To speak of a human "I" in Jesus is not to contradict the dogma of the divine and unique person into which the human nature of Jesus was assumed. On the other hand, to refuse Jesus a human "I" would be to deny the wholeness of his human nature. Cf. K. Rahner, *Aimer Jésus*, coll. "Jésus et Jésus Christ" (Paris: Desclée, 1985) 54–55.

135. Ex 12:16; Lev 23:3; Nm 29:1.

136. Cf. Ps 2:7; Heb 1:5.

137. Augustine, *De Civ. Dei* 17, 11. *CCL* 46, 575.

138. Jn 2:1–4; 19:25.

139. The account of Matthew 27:51–52 is more doctrinal than descriptive of a historical event.

140. It is a question of the descent of Jesus to Sheol, a subterranean place thought to be the abode of the dead, and not of a descent of Jesus to hell, the place of damnation, as the theory of substitution would have it (cf. above, p. 39).

141. It is Christ "brought to life in the spirit (the Spirit)" who goes to meet the spirits. The churches of the east represent Jesus' Resurrection with the icon of the descent into Sheol. Rightly so.

142. Although tradition has interpreted 1 Peter 3:18 as the meeting with the dead, this interpretation is not certain. Who are these "spirits"? The passage in 4:6 is more evident where it is truly to the dead that the Good News is brought.

143. The descent to this subterranean place, Sheol, is an image. Theology must uncover its meaning. In his glorifying death, Jesus became the Lord of all time. He goes to meet people in their death in order to introduce them into the kingdom. The first Christians thought only of those who died before Jesus' death. But still today the majority of people are in a time before Jesus Christ, since they have not heard him spoken of. Christians themselves are still in some way before the time of Jesus Christ. They are "in Christ," but not fully, called as they are "to the communion with the Son" in his day (cf. 1 Cor 1:7–9). It seems that the dogma of the descent of Jesus to Sheol, the grace of the encounter with him in death has value for every person. One can wish that the dogma of the descent of Jesus to the underworld will again attract the attention of theologians in order to clarify the mystery of death.

144. 2 Sam 7:12–16; Ps 45:7; 89:5, 30, 37.

145. Hag 2:23; Zech 3:8; 6:12.

146. To cite only Ps 2:2–7; 45:7; 110:1.

147. Hos 11:1; Mt 2:15.

Chapter 7

148. I am pleased to call to mind, among others, the works of two professors in Strasbourg: J. Schmitt, *Jésus ressuscité dans la prédication apostolique* (Paris: Gabalda, 1949); M. Deneken, *La Foi pascale* (Paris: Cerf, 1997).

149. In our days theology has gone beyond the definition of faith that was formerly current: the acceptance *by the intellect of revealed truths* because the person *wishes* to believe them, knowing them to be revealed. Such a faith does not demand an adherence to the person of Christ; it can be shared by demons (cf. Jas 2:19). These truths are accepted in their formulation without the person being aware of the mystery formulated. On the contrary, faith is a personal adherence and comprises an obscure but authentic knowledge.

150. Jn 1:16; Col 2:9–10.

151. "Humankind is justified by faith" alone and not by works (Rom 3:28). This principle is often interpreted this way: the person does not play any active role in his or her justification. This position is logical in a juridical theology where faith consists in believing that Christ paid the price, that God's justice takes it into account and justifies the person by reason of this faith. But faith embraces Christ and the salvation that is in him. The believer plays an active role, one of receptivity. Christ himself played this role in his death. On this point, juridical theology is incoherent: on the one hand, the justification of the person would be granted without participation on his or her part, whereas Christ would have had to acquire it by a work on behalf of humankind. The gift of totally gratuitous justification for humankind would not be such for the man Jesus. He embraced in himself the gift of justification for everyone. Truly he exercised causality of filial receptivity. It is the same for the believer in his or her communion with Christ.

152. *Letter* to *the Philippians*, 2. *SC* 10, 206.

153. In learned language: eschatology is also protology.

154. 1 Thess 4:11; cf. 1 Cor 15:19.

155. 1 Thess 1:3 pass. In 1 Corinthians 13:13 charity appears in third place because of its higher dignity.

156. The Holy Spirit is desire as much as it is love. The Spirit is a divine person who is love, and who is desire. The importance of desire in the life of a Christian is supreme. It is the manifestation of the presence of the Spirit. In the eyes of God the human person is worth his or her weight in desire. He or she believes and loves God in proportion to his or her sincere desire to believe and love.

157. Origin, *In Joh.*, 1. 10, c. 43, 305–306. *GCS* p. 222. "Today I believe in an imperfect manner, but one day there will come the perfect joy, and that which is imperfect will disappear. For faith by vision goes so infinitely far beyond the present faith that one can call it faith through a mirror and in enigma." It is to be noted that in speaking of seeing "distinctly, as in a mir-

ror" (1 Cor 13:12). Paul was not speaking of a mediate vision through reflection, but of a vision that is not precise like the mirrors of that era made it.

158. Charity is the force in the storm where the other two virtues would run the risk of sinking. It is those times when everything seems to contradict what one believes and hopes, when God does not seem to be Father or even real. But charity in communion with God makes one come alive. Nothing can overcome the communion in which one lives, no argument is of any worth against it. Thérèse of Lisieux said: "If you only knew in what darknesses I am lost! I no longer believe in eternal life. I think that after this mortal life there is nothing more, everything has disappeared for me. The only thing remaining to me is love." *Procès de l'ordinaire* (Rome: 1973) 402. The essential thing that contains faith and hope continued to remain with her.

159. Thomas Aquinas, *Com. in Rom* 8, 1. 1.

160. In declaring the faithful free of the law, Paul was thinking especially of the Mosaic law, but his thought extends to every law external to the person.

161. In antiquity, the guardian was a slave in charge of taking the child to school and of supervising his work.

162. 1 Cor 9:21; Gal 6:2.

163. The study of the paschal mystery has allowed a recentering of dogmatic theology that is surely beneficial. A similar recentering is desirable in moral theology that would not only free itself from modes of juridical thinking but, by taking everything fully into account, would subordinate the essentialist reflection in moral theology to a personalist way of thinking. Christian ethics would appear more as Good News, or an appeal that demands yet liberates the consciences of people. Then the role of conscience would also clearly come into prominence.

164. Vatican II, *Lumen Gentium,* 49.

165. For the "personalizer" role of the Spirit, I take the liberty of referring to my own work *L'Esprit Saint de Dieu* (Paris: Cerf, 1983) 37, 54, 94, 121, 132.

166. Cf. Col 1:13; Eph 2:6; Phil 3:20.

167. 1 Thess 5:12; Rom 12:28; 1 Tim 3:4–5; 5:17.

168. Heb 13:17; cf. 7:24.

169. Juridical type ecclesiology overtook the mystery of communion type ecclesiology at a time when a juridical theology of the redemption began to impose itself. No doubt that coincidence is not fortuitous.

170. Augustine, *De civitate Dei,* 10. *CCL* 47. 279.

171. Vatican II *Lumen Gentium,* 11. See W. M. Abbott (ed.), *The Documents of Vatican II* (New York: America/Association Press, 1966), 28.

172. The priest must be connected to the Church at least by the intention of doing what it does. Cf. Council of Trent, *Sess.* VII, Denzinger-Schönmetzer 1611. Ecclesial integration is fundamental.

173. Vatican II, *Lumen Gentium,* 28 declares that the priest acts *in persona Christi* but it does not say that he thus acts alone. *Presbyterorum Ordinis,* 2 makes explicit: "Priests...are so configured to Christ the Priest that they can act in the person of Christ the Head" (Abbott, 535). The priest is at the center and the summit of the ministry of the Church. If the faithful as well did not offer the Eucharist in the name of Christ, in whose name would they offer it?

174. Vatican II, *Lumen Gentium,* 32: "For the distinction which the Lord made between sacred ministers and the rest of the People of God entails a unifying purpose..." (Abbott, 58).

175. By distinguishing priests and other faithful by the fullness of ministry, one does not contradict Vatican II, *Lumen Gentium,* 10, that establishes that the common priesthood of the faithful and the ministerial or hierarchical priesthood "differ from one another in essence and not only in degree" (Abbott, 27). For in qualitative realities, therefore, not quantitative realities, the difference between fullness and what is not is specific. One can illustrate this difference by the image of a circle. Between the center and the circumference the difference is specific. However, the center is the circle itself in its total centering. In the priest the Church possesses its proper ministerial fullness.

176. In ecclesiology we must ensure that we pay exact attention to the words used. For example, it is better not to say that bishops are with and *under* Peter. Cf. "Lettre aux évêques de l'Église catholique sur certains aspects de l'Église envisagée comme communion," *Doc. cath.* 89 (1992) 73. The jurisdiction recognized in the pope over the whole Church and each of the faithful (Vatican I, Denzinger-Schönmetzer 3064) is not to be understood as similar to the power of an absolute monarch, but as the duty and the right to be effectively the *servus servorum Dei,* at the service of communion with the Holy Spirit. Those who want to grant the pope only a primacy of honor are mistaken: in the community, Jesus recognizes a primacy of service and not that of honor. An authority of service reverts to that primacy.

177. Thérèse of Lisieux said it forcefully: "I understood that love alone made the members of the Church act...I understood that love comprised all vocations." *Autobiographie, Oeuvres complètes* (Paris: Cerf, 1992), 226.

178. Cf. Irenaeus, *Adv. haer.* III, 241. *SC* 211, 475: the Spirit that springs from the side of Christ (Jn 7:37) springs from the body of Christ that is the Church.

179. The power of jurisdiction is an important reality of the Church on earth. But it must be exercised at the service of the mystery of communion. Great are the practical consequences that flow from it.

180. Cf. Vatican II, *Unitatis Redintegratio,* 6. John Paul II recognized that "an immense task" lies here. See the encyclical Ut *sint unum,* 96.

Chapter 8

181. Mt 10:1; 11:1; 14:19; 16:13.

182. J. Jeremias, *La dernière cene. Les paroles de Jésus* (translation; Paris: Cerf, 1972) 246–247.

183. Rev 12:1; 21:12–21.

184. Not only "called to be an apostle."

185. Hence there arises a certain way of understanding the distinction between priests and laity: some distribute and lead, others receive and follow.

186. The question is raised: in the allegory of the vine does it deal with the fruit of the virtues and good works, or with the fruit of the apostolate? It seems that one must get beyond these distinctions. As in John 4:34–38; 12:23–24, the fruit is that of Jesus' work collectively. In John 15:16, the promise of fruit is made to the disciple apostles. Faithfulness to Jesus through the virtues…is not the fruit but the condition for bearing fruit (Jn 15:4–5, 10). The allegory of the vine speaks of a community united to Jesus in which he bears fruit in the world.

187. Methodius of Olympus, *The Banquet*, 38, 77. SC 95, 106–108. The idea of spiritual maternity enlivened the courage of the martyrs of Lyons and Vienna. Cf. Eusebius, *Hist.* eccl., V, 1. SC 41, 6–23. Thérèse of Lisieux knew of the maternal vocation of the whole Church: "To be your spouse, O Jesus…(is) to be by my union with you the mother of souls (*Autobiographie. Oeuvres completes* (Paris: Cerf: 1992] 224).

188. Rev 1:2; 12:27 pass.

189. This "we" does not seem to be a "we" of majesty, referring to the sole author of the epistle, but of those who bear witness to Christ in the Church.

190. Cf. above, pp. 31–34.

191. Augustine, *In Joh.*, tract. 47, 3. CCL 36, 405–406.

192. Idem, *Sermo 354. PL* 39, 1563.

193. Idem, *In Joh.*, tract. 35, 4. CCL 36, 319, 405.

194. Vatican II, *Lumen Gentium* 48; *Sacrosanctum Concilium* 5; *Apostolicam Actuositatem* 5; *Gaudium et Spes* 45.

195. This description can appear a caricature. But a caricature possesses its proper truth which is to emphasize excessively its authentic characteristics.

196. Vatican II, *Presbyterorum Ordinis*, 5.

197. It is not to be translated: "set apart to announce the gospel" but for the gospel itself that is the mystery of salvation in its propagation.

198. "The being set apart for the gospel" (Rom 1:1) is a consecration according to biblical language. Cf. Lev 20:26.

199. It is not to be translated: "I have fully ensured the proclamation of the gospel" (Traduction Oecumdénique de la Bible). Through Paul, there is recognized a mystery that is the gospel.

200. The sense of totality expressed by opposing contraries becomes evident in Luke 6:9: "Is it lawful to do good on the sabbath rather than to do evil, to save life rather than to destroy it?" It is evidently not permitted to do evil. The sense is: is it forbidden to do whatever, even to save a life? The Church did not receive the power to keep a person in sin. Jesus himself did not receive such power—he who came not to condemn but to save (cf. Jn 3:17; 10:10).

201. By baptism according to the interpretation of Saint Cyprian, *Ep.* 73, 7. *CSEL* III, 783. By the sacrament of penance/reconciliation according to the Council of Trent, Sess. XIV, Can. 2, Denzinger-Schönmetzer 1703. The council condemns the interpretation that saw in John 20:21–23 only the mission of proclaiming the forgiveness of sins acquired by the cross without acknowledging the Church's power to forgive them. It is not opposed to the exegesis that is common today that sees here the global mission of the Church to forgive sins.

202. One sees how the pastoral of the sacrament of penance/reconciliation can be dynamized by its understanding of the sacrament of evangelization, of conversion, and how much it is required for the ministers of this sacrament. The Church must be an agent of conversion, especially in its ministers.

203. Cf. above, pp. 31–34.

204. The Traduction Oecuménique de la Bible renders the eucharistic allusion well: "I will take supper with him."

205. Cf. J. Jeremias, *La dernière cène. Les paroles de Jésus* (translation; Paris Cerf, 1972) 302. The finality that destines Jesus for the second coming is in his death itself.

206. From the first centuries the celebration of the Eucharist began with a commented reading of Scripture.

207. They did not recognize him "at the breaking of the bread," in the manner of breaking it, but "in," that is, during the breaking of the bread in the meal that is so-called.

208. May I be permitted to devote a more developed reflection on these two questions, for even nowadays many theologians do not explain the paschal mystery whose sacrament it is?

209. From that time the Eucharist appears less like "the table of the Lord" (1 Cor 10:21) where one shares in the paschal mystery than as an altar on which a priest again sacrifices a victim. The faithful "assisted" at the sacrifice of the Mass but rarely received communion there. What is more, the distinction between priests and lay people was understood after the manner of separation: on the one hand, the priest who alone sacrifices; on the other hand, the faithful who assist at the sacrifice. The Eucharist is the sacrament of the unique sacrifice of Christ; the Church offers this unique sacrifice by joining itself to it thanks to this sacrament.

210. The prayer over the gifts that is said on Holy Thursday and the Second Sunday in Ordinary Time. The primitive tenor of this very ancient prayer was

according to M. C. Mohlbert, *Sacramentarium Veronense* VIII, XXV, 93, Rome, 1956, p. 16: *Quoties-cumque hujus hostiae commemoratio celebratur, opus nostrae redemptionis exseritur*—the work of our redemption takes place exteriorly, gushes out, emerges.

211. At least in the west.

212. This theory had the great merit of surmounting this dilemma: either simple presence signified by the bread (Berengar of Tours) or presence similar to that of an earthly body where the body of Christ is "touched and broken by the hands of the priests and ground by the teeth of the faithful." Denzinger-Schönmetzer 690.

213. Those who hold this theory call attention to the absence of any analogy between the Eucharist understood by them and the mystery of the Incarnation. In being Man/God, Jesus remains an authentic human, but the bread ceases to be bread when it becomes Eucharist.

214. "The giving of meaning" practiced by human beings is only transitory. Should the young woman (cf. above) drop the bouquet, the cow will come and eat what is only a plant. In the logic of the theory of transignification, the consecrated but not consumed hosts or wine in the celebration are sometimes brought back to the sacristy like ordinary bread and wine, since there is no one any longer to give them a Eucharistic meaning.

215. According to the scholastic explanation there is no longer either bread or wine in the Eucharist. There only remain their accidents without the substance of the bread and wine. According to the theory of transignification, the meaning can be totally changed. For example, the bouquet that is offered (cf. above) is no longer at all a plant for grazing. On the contrary, the bread becomes the most genuine bread there is, bread that one eats and that nourishes humans in their entirety for the final resurrection. Hence it is bread whose meaning is not abolished but reinforced and broadened.

216. *Adv. haer.* IV, 18, 5; cf. V, 2, 3. *SC* 100, 611–613; 153, 35–37. Ambrose, *De Sacram.* 4, 16. *SC* 25 bis, 11: "Before the consecration it is not the body of Christ, but after the consecration I tell you that it is the body of Christ. He said and it was done; he has commanded and it was created. You yourself existed, but you are an old creature; after you were consecrated, you began to be a new creature." Augustine, *Sermo* 272, *PL* 38, 1246–1248: "It is your own sacramental sign that is on the table of the Lord; you receive the sacramental sign of that which you are....Be then truly what you are and receive what you are." See also Gregory of Nyssa, *Or. cat.* 37, 3, *PG* 45, 93–96.

217. *De Paschate. PL* 67, 1053–1059.

218. Analogy means similarity and difference. Great is the similarity between the Eucharist and the Church. Great also is the difference. A Christian is a person and a freedom. Bread and wine are not that. Christ can assimilate them to himself without resistance, instantaneously and entirely, as material means of his presence to the world.

219. *Apology*, 66.
220. On the subject of the consecration of the bread and the wine explained by the paschal mystery whose sacrament is the Eucharist, I take the liberty of referring to my work *L'Eucharistie, sacrement pascal* (Paris: Cerf, 1980).

Chapter 9

221. Every "external work," such as creation, is common to the three Persons. However, the work is trinitarian—in the common work each person plays his role.
222. Mt 26:64 & par.; Acts 7:55; Rom 8:34; Eph 1:20; Col 3:1; Heb 1:3; 10:12; 12:2; 1 Pet 3:22.
223. Ps 104:30; 33:6; Job 34:16–17.
224. Cf. below, chapter eleven.
225. Thomas Aquinas, *Prol. in II Sent.*
226. The death with which humanity is threatened because of its disobedience (Gen 2:17) is not simple physical death, but the one that cuts it off from God, the source of life.
227. One usually places Christianity among the religions of the book. But Christianity is not such after the manner of Islam or even Judaism. Sacred Scripture has a supreme importance in Christianity but itself attests that Jesus is greater than what all the books in the world could say about him (Jn 21:25). Before all else, Christians read Jesus Christ. They read him by joining themselves to him, especially in the celebration of the Eucharist.
228. One ordinarily translates: "Everything is created for him." The Greek preposition *eis* designates a movement toward Christ. Paul likewise says about Christ: "Through whom all things are and through [*eis*] whom we exist" (1 Cor 8:6).
229. Rom 4:17. Cf. Isa 41:4; 48:13; Ezek 36:29; Wis 11:25.
230. The Demonstration of the Apostolic Teaching, 72, *SC* 406, 101.
231. Augustine, *Sermo* 337. *In dedic. Ecclesiae. PL* 38, 1477.
232. The same idea, it seems, inspires Hebrews 1:2. Often the question is posed: Would the Incarnation have taken place if humanity had not sinned? That question is unanswerable. Only God knows what he would have done. But knowing what he has done, we see that God wishes to lead sinful humanity to its filial dignity, creating it in his Son and toward him.
233. "Image of God"—cf. Col 1:15; 2 Cor 3:18; 4:5. "Firstborn"—cf. Col 1:15; Rom 8:29; Col 1:18. "In him"—cf. Col 1:16; 1 Cor 1:30. "Toward him"—cf. Col 1:16; Rom 6:3; 1 Cor 1:9; 12:13.
234. Speaking in this way, one does not deny, indeed one affirms the doctrine of sin that weighs on humanity from the beginning.

235. As it would be too unjust to cast into hell infants who died without baptism, who, therefore, were not able to enter the order of salvation, this theology had imagined "the limbo of the infants." The latter, excluded from salvation by reason of original sin, would, however, be exempt from the pains of hell, enjoying a "natural happiness."

236. Vatican II, *Lumen Gentium* 13: "All men are called to be part of this catholic unity of the People of God....And there belong to it or are related to it in various ways..." (Abbott, 32).

237. If a person does not have the possibility to have recourse to the ordinary means of salvation, it is up to God to provide another means for such a person. Vatican II, *Lumen Gentium* 22, 5 declares: "Since Christ died for all and the final vocation of humanity is truly unique, namely divine, we have to hold that the Holy Spirit offers the possibility of being associated with the paschal mystery in a way that God alone knows."

238. Irenaeus, *Adv. haer.* V, 18, 3. *SC* 153, 245.

Chapter 10

239. Regarding death, it is necessary to distinguish the biological aspect and the human, personal aspect that is the fulfillment of human destiny.

240. This translation, however, is not certain. One could punctuate the sentence in another way: "So too will God, through Jesus, bring with him those who have fallen asleep." The translation given above seems more probable to us. In any case, the faithful are "in Christ" (1 Thess 4:16), "in the Lord" (Rev 14:13).

241. The Greek text expresses well the unity between death and eternal life with Christ. The same article governs both verbs in the infinitive: "I long to depart this life and be with Christ."

242. To be sure, God rewards merits. But let us recall that to merit is not to give to God, it is to receive his gifts.

243. Mk 1:8; Jn 16:7–11.

244. Cf. above, pp. 31–34.

245. Rom 8:34; Heb 7:25.

246. Council of Trent, *Sess.* XXV. Denzinger-Schönmetzer 1820.

247. As a matter of fact, the existence of the separated soul is no longer a real human existence. Thomas Aquinas, *Super epist. s. Pauli Lectura.* Ed. VIII revisa. Vol. 1, 411: *Anima mea non est ego:* "My soul is not identical with my 'I.'" *S. Th.* IIa IIae, q. 83, a. 11, ad 5: "Peter's soul is not Peter." *S. Th.* Ia, q. 29, a. 1., ad 5: "The soul is only a part of man....Hence neither the definition nor the name of person is suitable to him."

248. J. Ratzinger, *La Foi chrétienne hier* et *aujourd'hui.* Coll. "Tradition chrétienne." (Translation: Paris: Cerf, 1985) 253: "Immortality does not simply result from a natural nonpossibility of death, proper to the indivisible being; it

comes from the saving action of someone who loves us and who has the necessary power."

249. Jn 11:25; 14:6.

250. Thérèse of Lisieux, *Lettre 244. Oeuvres complètes* (Paris: Cerf, 1992) 601.

251. In this obscure text the dwelling prepared in heaven that one will put on in death does not seem to be without a relationship to Christ who puts on.

252. Phil 3:20; 1 Thess 1:10.

253. 1 Cor 15:43–44; Phil 3:21.

254. The action of the Spirit personalizes. Cf. above, p. 98, note #165.

255. Mt 25:31–46 is a picturesque description, a parable of the last judgment.

256. Cf. above, p. 25, note #46.

257. Lk 11:20; 17:21.

258. One has sometimes interpreted 1 Corinthians 15:24–28 as an abdication of sovereignty when Christ would reenter the common ranks. Cf. the work that previously attracted a large audience: O. Cullmann, *Le Christ et le temps* (Neuchâtel: Delachaux et Niestlé, 1947) 107; idem, *Christologie du N. T.* (Neuchâtel: Delachaux et Niestlé, 1958) 195. This interpretation follows the logic of those theologies in which redemption is only a function of Christ and is not situated in his filial relationship with God. From that perspective, the mystery of the Incarnation can be regarded as an interlude and not as the zenith of God's action in the world.

259. Acts 13:52; Rom 14:17; Gal 5:22; 1 Thess 1:6.

Chapter 11

260. Rom 1:4 ("the resurrection of the dead according to the Spirit of holiness"); 8:11, 23; 1 Cor 15:44.

261. Rom 6:4; 2 Cor 13:2; Phil 3:21; 1 Cor 15:43–44.

262. Irenaeus, *Adv. haer.* III, 18, 3. *SC* 211, 350–351. Basil, *On the Holy Spirit*, 28. *SC* 17, 156.

263. He is the force of the Gospel that arouses faith (Rom 15:18–19; 1 Thess 1:5).

264. Cyril of Alexandria, *Thesaurus assert.* 34. *PG* 75, 580, 608.

265. "To pour out the Spirit" and "outpouring of the Spirit" are typical phrases for the gift of the Spirit. Cf. Isa 32:15; Ezek 36:25–27; Joel 2:28; Zech 12:10; Acts 2:17–18, 33; 10:45; Titus 3:6.

266. Cf. 2 Cor 1:22; Eph 1:13–14.

267. Cf. Rom 8:4 and Eph 5:2; Rom 15:16 and Eph 1:4; Eph 2:22; 4:16; Col 2:2.

268. 2 Cor 13:13; Phil 2:1.

269. 1 Cor 12:13; cf. Eph 4:4.

270. Because God is entirely love according to 1 John 4:8, many authors refuse to see in charity a personal character of the Spirit. That objection is futile. Other attributes of what is called "divine nature" are personalized in the Spirit, such as holiness and power. The Father loves, the Son also loves, the Spirit is

Love. As such, it is the Spirit of the Father who begets by loving, of the Son who by loving lets himself be begotten.

271. Probably under the influence of Greek thought.

272. See above, pp. 31–34.

273. Basil, *On the Holy Spirit*, 9. *SC* 17, 145.

274. For the use of this term, see above, p. 16–17.

275. By the etymology of the word and the notion that one developed of holiness. Cf. Lev 20:24.

276. See above, p. 47.

277. See above, p. 1.

278. One can conclude from this that in God's plan death is not an evil, but can become a privileged place for the creative action of the Spirit. One misinterprets Scripture when one states that humanity is only mortal by reason of sin.

279. Cf. the doxology of the eucharistic prayer.

280. God is neither one nor three according to the meaning of these numbers that are mutually exclusive.

281. E. Jacob, *La Théologie de l'Ancien Testament* (Neuchâtel: Delachaux et Niestlé, 1955) 100.

282. *De Fide* et *Symbolo* 1, 19. *CCL* 50 A, 523–524.

283. Master Eckhart, *Sermo* 11. *Impletum est tempus Elisabeth*, Meister Eckhart's Predigten, I. (Stuttgart: Kohlhammer, 1958) 177, 472.

284. Rom 8:15; Gal 4:4–6; cf. Jn 3:5.

285. There would be every reason to study this affinity at greater length to explore the mystery of the Spirit, the meaning of Christ's death and of death such as it is in the plan of creation. I point out the work of J. Kockerols, *L'Esprit à la Croix* (Brussels: Ed. Lessius, 1999).

286. Mystagogical, that is, admitting one to the knowledge of the mystery.

287. Mt 11:27; Jn 7:29; 8:55.

288. If theology could not move from the economy to the eternal mystery, would it have the right to teach that the mystery is Trinitarian, that the three are Persons, that the one proceeds from such another, that they are of equal majesty…?

289. The Church that is born of the Passover of Christ is not added to the paschal mystery. It is contained in it. The Church is born with and in Christ whom the Father raises in the Holy Spirit.

290. Augustine, *De Trinitate*, 8, 14. *CCL* 50, 290.

291. Gregory of Nazianzus, *Oration* 31, 8. *SC* 250, 290: "The Spirit is a middle term between the Unbegotten and the Begotten."

292. Following Photius who compares the Trinity to a balance whose two scales represent the Son and the Spirit: *Amphilogia*, Q 181. *PG* 191, 846.

293. The Holy Spirit would make up for this intra-Trinitarian sterility by an un-

limited fecundity in creation and the Church. Cf., for example, P. de Bérulle, *Grandeurs de Jésus,* IV, 2. See M. Dupuy, "L'Esprit Saint et Marie dans l'école fraçaise," *Études mariales* 26 (1969) 27.

294. When, on the contrary, one says that the Father begets the Son on the one hand, and breathes forth the Spirit on the other hand, or that the Father breathes forth the Spirit through the Son, does one not run the risk of making the Spirit like a "second Son," since the Father is essentially Father?

295. Jn 3:5; cf. Titus 3:5.

296. The theories where the Spirit proceeds after the begetting of the Son ignore the quasi-maternal role of the Spirit.

297. The preposition "of" characterizes the role of the Spirit and that of the women in Matthew's genealogy (1:3, 5, 6, 16, 18, 20).

298. Maximilian Kolbe, *L'Immaculée révèle l'Esprit Saint. Entretiens spirituels inédits.* Translated by J. F. Villepelée. (Paris: Lethilleux, 1974) 48.

299. According to the famous axiom: *Non coerceri maximo, contineri autem minimo, divinum est.*